W9-CAZ-127

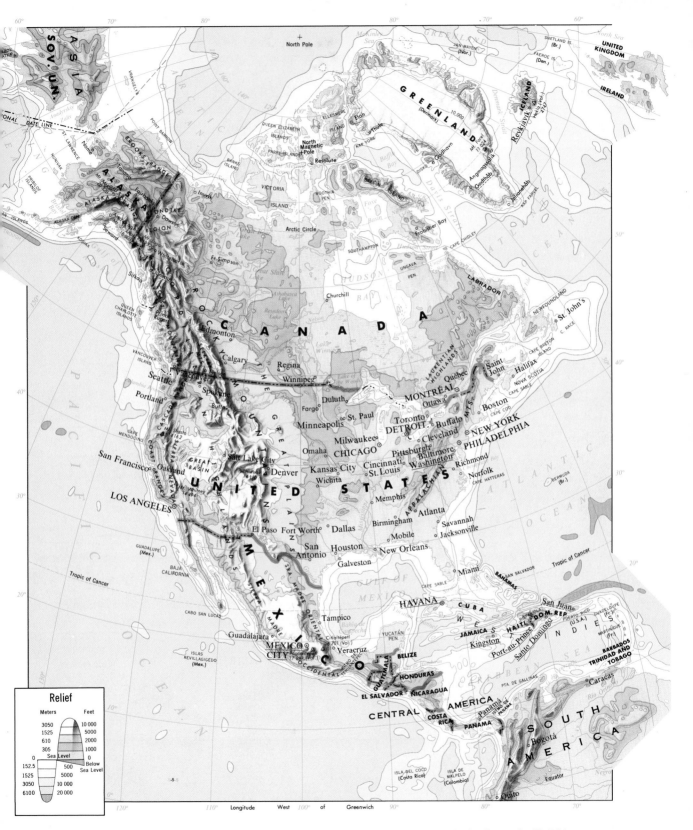

Map from Cosmopolitan World Atlas,
© 1995 by Rand McNally, 94-S-265

Map from Goode's World Atlas,
© 1995 by Rand McNally, 94-S-265

Enchantment of the World

HONDURAS

by Harry R. Targ and Marlene Targ Brill

Consultant for Honduras: George I. Blanksten, Ph.D., Professor Emeritus of Political Science, Northwestern University, Evanston, Illinois

Consultant for Reading: Robert L. Hillerich, Ph.D., Professor Emeritus, Bowling Green State University; Pinellas County Schools, Florida

CHILDRENS PRESS ®

CHICAGO

Bananas are loaded onto a cable and pulled to the packing plant.

Project Editor: Mary Reidy
Design: Margrit Fiddle
Photo Research: Feldman & Associates, Inc.

Library of Congress Cataloging-in-Publication Data

Targ, Harry R.
  Honduras / by Harry R. Targ and Marlene Targ Brill.
    p.   cm.—(Enchantment of the world)
  Includes index.
  Summary: Discusses the geography, history, government,
economics, people, and culture of this poor Central
American country.
  ISBN 0-516-02635-6
  1. Honduras—Juvenile literature. [1. Honduras.]
I. Brill, Marlene Targ. II. Title. III. Series.
F1503.2.T37 1995   95-2689
972.83—dc20   CIP
                                                 AC

Copyright © 1995 by Childrens Press®, Inc.
All rights reserved. Published simultaneously in Canada.
Printed in the United States of America.
  2 3 4 5 6 7 8 9 10 R 04 03 02 01 00 99 98 97 96

Picture Acknowledgments
Art Museum of the Americas: 87
The Bettmann Archive: 30, 33, 41, 49, 93 (left)
Lee Boltin Picture Library: © Andrew Courtney, 74, 77, 83,
88 (left), 94 (bottom left), 109 (left)
D. Donne Bryant Stock: © Brenda J. Latvala, 9, 64, 66 (left),
92 (right); © Max & Bea Hunn, 11, 85 (right), 86 (right), 90;

© **J.P. Courau,** 14, 20 (top), 101, 108; © **Stewart Aitchison,**
18, 22, 103 (left); © **Chris R. Sharp,** 32, 34, 35; © **James D.
Nations,** 53, 97; © **Cleo Photography,** 62; © **Mark R.
Valentino,** 66 (right); © **Byron Augustin,** 68 (inset), 79, 85
(left), 86 (left), 94 (bottom right), 99; © **Michael Everett,** 82,
93 (right); © **Daniel Komer,** 102; © **Donald Bryant,** 107
© **Victor Englebert:** 102 (inset)
H. Armstrong Roberts: © Englebert/Zefa, 104 (inset)
Chip and Rosa Maria de la Cueva Peterson: 4, 8, 12, 15,
23, 37, 52 (2 photos), 59 (2 photos), 92 (left), 100
Photri: 43, 75; © **Marka Photos,** 5; © **John Clark,** 106
© **Carl Purcell:** 96
Reuters/Bettmann: 60 (2 photos), 88 (right)
Root Resources: © Mary A. Root, 38
Tom Stack & Associates: © Byron Augustin, 13, 68, 72, 94
(top)
Tony Stone Images: © Robert E. Daemmrich, 81, 98 (left);
© Peter Poulides, 103 (right); © Norbert Wu, 104
SuperStock International, Inc.: 44, 98 (right); © Max W.
Hunn, 6
Unicorn Stock Photos: © Alon Reininger 16, 20 (bottom)
UPI/Bettmann Newsphotos: 55 (2 photos), 70
Valan: © Jean Marie Jro, Cover; © Albert Kuhnigk, 25 (left);
© Stephen J. Krasemann, 25 (top right), 26 (bottom left and
right), 27 (center); © Jeff Foott, 25 (bottom right), 26 (top
left); © John Cancalosi, 27 (left)
Visuals Unlimited: © Milton H. Tierney, Jr., 19, 65; © Joe
McDonald, 27 (right); © G. Prance, 28; © David Matherly,
109 (right)
Len W. Meents: Maps on 91, 99, 103, 108
**Courtesy Flag Research Center, Winchester,
Massachusetts 01890:** Flag on back cover
Cover: View of Tegucigalpa

Flower vendors on their way to the market in Tegucigalpa

TABLE OF CONTENTS

Chapter 1

THE FORGOTTEN

COUNTRY

Travelers enter Honduras along the new Inter-Ocean Highway. The glistening road links the two major cities of Tegucigalpa and San Pedro Sula in northwest Honduras. At first glance Honduras looks like a prosperous country. Lush, forested mountains surround the two cities dotted with sprinkles of modern government and office buildings. Business people in contemporary dress move slowly through their work day.

But far from the highway lie *asentimientos*, "settlements." These secluded villages are home to the majority of Hondurans. They are poor rural farmers who seem forgotten by time and the outside world. Most of Honduras is hidden, as it has been for centuries.

CENTRAL AMERICA'S HIDDEN REGION

Until the 1980s, little was known about Honduras outside Central America. Similar origins blurred boundaries and information about countries in the entire region. Today, Honduras

Opposite page: In Tegucigulpa houses are built up the slopes of Mount Picacho.

The head of a sun god found at Copán

nestles in the middle of the seven Central American nations (Belize, Guatemala, El Salvador, Honduras, Nicaragua, Costa Rica, and Panama) and halfway between North America and South America. Even with this central location, Honduras developed many features distinct from its neighbors that make the country important to study.

Between A.D. 250 and the 1520s, Maya Indians populated Central America. The province of Copán in western Honduras was the site of many advanced scientific Mayan discoveries. The Honduran Indian Lempira led one of the largest rebellions in Central America against Spanish colonists during the 1500s. After his death the entire region fell to Spain.

The area that is now Honduras had been the first point on the continents of North and South America reached by Christopher Columbus. The explorer arrived at what is now the port at

The Spanish fort of San Fernando de Omoa was built in the second half of the eighteenth century.

Trujillo in 1502. He headed southeast along the northern Honduran coast, which he called *Gracias a Díos*, "Thanks to God." The name reflects how grateful Columbus was that his ships had weathered the wild storms. When the sea calmed, Columbus named the region *Honduras*, meaning "depths," to thank God for saving his ships from the depths of the storm.

Spanish colonists followed and built strongholds throughout Central America. Spain ruled the region from the 1500s until it gained independence in the 1820s. From 1827 to 1839 Honduran General Francisco Morazán led the newly independent Central American states, which formed the United Provinces of Central America. Morazán struggled to keep this federation alive as one government. The countries that made up the Central American Federation eventually went their separate ways, but several Honduran leaders have kept the dream of a united Central America alive to this day.

Various powers fought for control within the nations surrounding Honduras. Governments changed frequently and violently. Armies fought against their own citizens. The nations allowed foreign governments to interfere with local control.

Hondurans, however, kept to themselves and solved their own problems. Well into the twentieth century Honduras was known to the outside world mainly for its banana exports. Without significant outside investors, Honduras remained poor and underdeveloped, with a weak government and army.

Yet unlike their neighbors, proud Hondurans knew how to organize for change peacefully. When banana plantation workers protested conditions during the 1950s, the Honduran government passed labor laws to protect workers' rights. Poor peasants gained land reforms that were unusual for the region, even though these rights were often ignored. Because the government was weak, peasants experienced less violence than in neighboring countries.

During the 1980s outside forces altered the peaceful and isolated Honduran way of life. Honduras's central location meant the country was close to the fighting in Nicaragua, El Salvador, and Guatemala. The United States built military bases in Honduras to train soldiers from neighboring Nicaragua to fight against their government and soldiers from El Salvador to fight against a popular rebellion. Honduran governments with strong armies backed by the United States never became as violent as these nearby countries. But the country that was once forgotten by most of the world suddenly made news.

Some Hondurans welcomed the foreign soldiers and their money. Others found foreigners a threat to their way of life. Neither side realized that the military bases would thrust their small, sparsely populated country into the international spotlight.

A campesino family

LIFE IN HONDURAS

Honduras has a small wealthy class, a large poor class, and a smaller group of people in between. But the divisions between rich and poor are less extreme here than in other Central American countries. Large corporations that support the slow-growing industries are mainly foreign owned. Because most business profits flow out of the country, less is left for wealthy lifestyles.

Most Hondurans are *campesinos*, or rural peasants. More than 57 percent of the campesinos live in villages away from main roads. The distance from cities limits their influence on politics, religion, and the economy.

Campesino families live in one-room homes called *ranchos*. The ranchos are made of bamboo, sugarcane or corn stalks, and mud.

One-room ranchos *near Puerto Cortés*

Overhead are roofs of tightly sewn cane. A cloth hangs from the ceiling to divide the room. Dirt floors, polluted water, gaslights, and mosquitoes are part of everyday life.

Few campesinos can afford furnishings. A wood-burning stove sits in the kitchen portion. Separated sections of a rancho hold a bed for the parents and a place for children to sleep. Beds are mats on the floor or hammocks. Other furniture may be a table and chairs or tree stumps to sit on.

Peasants work long hours just to provide enough food to eat. The majority of rural campesinos are either small farmers with their own land or landless workers who earn wages on plantations or smaller farms. More often, men who own small plots also work their fathers' land and obtain part-time jobs to add to their family's earnings. Many workers must leave home and travel to plantations at harvest time. Even then, earnings barely reach $1.50 to $2.50 U.S. per day.

A small cabbage farm

Those who have land plant corn, rice, and beans—the main campesino foods. Harvested crops serve as a source of meals. Any extra produce is sold at market. Money from crops pays for medicine, clothing, and foods that are not grown locally, such as chili peppers, bananas, mangoes, or papayas.

When families have an emergency, such as an illness, they must sell their food to get money. Clinics are so far away that workers lose a day's wages just for travel. If families need to buy food in town, the cost is often much greater than what they earn from their own crops. Therefore, poor people never seem to get ahead.

Each day brings many physical challenges. Women awake before dawn to grind the corn for tortillas, a round flat bread, and prepare coffee. During the day women care for children, tend the family's animals, wash clothes in a stream, iron and mend tattered clothes, and bargain in the market for used clothing. Church and social groups from foreign countries donate some clothes. A

All these tobacco workers are children. They are preparing tobacco leaves for drying.

common sight is children wearing donated T-shirts sporting names from summer camps in the United States.

Children accompany their mothers into the mountains to gather firewood for cooking. After bringing men their lunch in the fields, many women and children join the men at work. They dig the fields with hoes or *machetes* (large heavy knives), plow land, and chop wood. Because campesino children help earn money for food, they rarely have time for play or to attend school. In the city or larger villages, children from poor families help their parents fill tortillas to sell on street corners.

Teenagers from poorer families must always be alert in the city at night. Soldiers snatch teens from the streets at gunpoint to be military recruits. Often teenagers disappear without a word. Eventually their families receive a letter saying they have joined the army.

Families of businesspersons, landowners, military officers, and professional workers have easier lifestyles. The children go to

Schoolgirls

school, enjoy toys and team sports, and live in homes with electricity and running water. Their diets include pork, beef, eggs, and a variety of tropical fruits and vegetables. Adults have time and money for leisure activities, such as eating at restaurants, dancing at discos, or surfing. Wealthier Hondurans travel on paved roads in expensive cars, often passing campesinos on horseback or foot.

Small clusters of urban Hondurans have a lifestyle somewhere in between that of these two groups. Their homes have cement floors and tiled roofs. Some houses have two or three rooms plus a separate kitchen. Larger towns may have electricity, running water, and schools and stores. Townsfolk take advantage of new jobs in government, trade, or manufacturing. Like campesinos, they organize to protect their rights as workers.

Because Honduras has had strong peasant and workers' movements and the government has been weak, conflict and violence have been less than elsewhere in Central America.

The rugged mountains of Honduras have affected the country's economy and government throughout its history.

Chapter 2

THE DIVIDED LAND

Local artists draw pictures of an ideal rural Honduras. The scenes show peaceful mountains and colorful tropical forests. People in these drawings work this lush land as they have for centuries.

Yet the same land that gives to the people also has limited the country's progress. Geography plays an important role in how Hondurans live. The government and economy have suffered through the years because of the rough mountains that spread across the country. Honduras has less land available for farming than other Central American countries. Mountainous land with deep ravines isolates settlements and traps rural Hondurans in another time. Forested mountains separate the low, level northern seacoast from the Pacific coast in the south. The mountains split the eastern provinces from the rest of the country.

LOCATION

Honduras is the second largest of the seven Central American countries. The cone-shaped nation is about the size of Tennessee

A quiet beach on a small island in the Caribbean Sea

in the United States. Its 43,277 square miles (112,088 square kilometers) are located halfway between North and South America.

An important factor for trade was Honduras's position between two major bodies of water. The northern coastline stretches along the Caribbean Sea for 382 miles (615 kilometers). To the southwest, Honduras has a 48-mile (77-kilometer) coastline on the Pacific Ocean at the Gulf of Fonseca.

Honduras shares its largest land border with Nicaragua to the south. The boundary extends 490 miles (789 kilometers). The northwest border with Guatemala spans 210 miles (338 kilometers). Honduras's southwest boundary with El Salvador also runs 210 miles (338 kilometers).

Tropical rain forest

REGIONS

Honduras consists of five main areas. The interior highlands comprise about two-thirds of the country. Thick rain forests cover most of these mountains. Highland mountains zigzag without any special pattern, so the rough ground is difficult to cultivate. Early villages were mining towns, like the capital Tegucigalpa. Gradually, small farm and livestock communities developed in a number of mountain valleys. Soil was richer in the western and central portions of the highland valleys. Today, the region supports 70 percent of the population.

The Pacific lowlands form an uneven strip at the base of the mountains along the Gulf of Fonseca. Coastal plains cover about 2 percent of the land. Tropical rain forests give way to rich savanna pastures, treeless flatlands covered with grasses. The largest plain

Above: Cattle graze on lowlands near the coast.
Below: A fishing boat from a small village in the Gulf of Fonseca

surrounds the Choluteca River. Coastline pastures are valuable for raising livestock, such as mules and cattle, and farming.

Hondurans call the Caribbean lowlands, or North Coast, *La Costa*. The North Coast is the site of the most active economic growth in the country. Its fertile plains and numerous river valleys offer rich farming. Farmers grow lemons, oranges, grapefruit, and pineapples for export. Banana companies produce the greatest crops in the Ulúa-Chamelecón River basin and the western coastal plain. Some farming exists east of the city of Tela. San Pedro Sula, the region's busy market city, is the country's leading commercial center and gateway to the interior valleys. The North Coast contains the three major ports of Tela, La Ceiba, and Puerto Cortés, the country's main port.

The coastal plains in the northeast are called *La Mosquitia*, "Mosquito Coast." Steamy tropical rain forests blanket much of this region. Several narrow river valleys push inland. Only a few small Indian towns populate the area, which lies largely undeveloped. Mosquito Coast forests and grasslands are said to hold many untapped resources.

Honduras governs a number of small islands in the Caribbean Ocean and Gulf of Fonseca. The Swan Islands are two small islands 125 miles (201 kilometers) to the north in the Caribbean.

About 38 miles (61 kilometers) offshore are *Islas de la Bahía*, "the Bay Islands." These islands form a 78-mile (126-kilometer) arc in the Caribbean. They spring from undersea peaks of the mainland Omoa Mountains. Bay Island mountains reach 1,300 feet (396 meters) and are covered with dense forests. Once the islands were home to African slaves and English pirates. Now a mixture of residents who are descendants of French, English, and African people play host to a trickle of tourists pursuing water sports off the beautiful coral reefs.

A coral reef surrounds one of the small offshore islands.

LANDFORMS AND WATERWAYS

Rugged mountains and narrow coastal plains surrounding rivers describe most of Honduran geography. Mountains of varying heights cover almost 80 percent of Honduras. The highest point reaches 9,400 feet (2,865 meters) in the Cerros de Celaque, a mountain range that sweeps across northern Honduras. Pico Bonito soars more than 8,000 feet (2,438 meters) above the town of La Ceiba. The main mountain ranges include the Cordillera Opalaca in the west, Montañas de Comayagua to the south, and Montañas del Patuca reaching eastward.

Honduras lacks the active volcanoes found in other Central American countries. With coarse terrain and without volcanic ash to enrich the soil, farming is poor. However, several mountain plateaus provide enough fertile soil for farming.

Honduras has many streams, rivers, and coastal lagoons with

The Río Lempa in the southwest section of Honduras

coral reefs. The Ulúa River extends over 180 miles (290 kilometers). It meets the Chamelecón River to drain from northern mountains onto the Sula plain, leaving fertile soil. The Goascoran, Choluteca, and Nacaome Rivers flow into the Pacific Ocean to the south.

Major waterways along the Caribbean are the Coco and Patuca. The Coco River stretches the farthest across Honduras along the Nicaraguan border. Its 500 miles (805 kilometers) flow through wetlands and forests of the Mosquito Coast. The powerful Patuca River is known for its lovely waterfalls. Both rivers were once pathways for pirates and English explorers. Today they provide travel in areas where there are few roads.

Several waterways are navigable for small ships. Hondurans especially value Lake Yojoa in the Xicaque Mountains. Lake Yojoa lies between the two main cities of Tegucigalpa and San Pedro Sula at 2,100 feet (640 meters) above sea level. The lake is 12 miles (19 kilometers) long and 7 miles (11 kilometers) wide.

CLIMATE

Honduran weather varies with mountain elevation and nearness to the seas. Tropical heat cools farther up the mountains. Sometimes short distances produce dramatic changes in temperature and rainfall. Temperatures are pleasantly warm somewhere in Honduras any day of the year.

Lowland temperatures are always hot. The average annual temperature remains a constant 88 degrees Fahrenheit (31 degrees Celsius). Highland regions have milder weather. Central Honduras has moderate temperatures of about 59 to 68 degrees Fahrenheit (15 to 20 degrees Celsius). In Tegucigalpa, 3,070 feet (936 meters) above sea level, the average temperature is 74 degrees Fahrenheit (23 degrees Celsius).

The entire country shares two seasons. A rainy season lasts from May to October, with temperatures averaging 59 degrees Fahrenheit (15 degrees Celsius) in the west and 86 degrees Fahrenheit (30 degrees Celsius) in the north. A dry season prevails from November to April, with 75 degrees Fahrenheit (24 degrees Celsius) in the highlands, 73 degrees Fahrenheit (23 degrees Celsius) in the west, and 86 degrees Fahrenheit (30 degrees Celsius) in the south. (Along the coast the term dry season means only that rainfall is less rather than that the season is totally dry.) In the rainy season strong winds blow from the northeast, bringing unusual amounts of moisture from the shore. Tropical rain forests receive more than 100 inches (254 centimeters) of rain per year. Hurricanes often are a problem. In 1974 Hurricane Fifi cost Honduras ten thousand lives and $1 million in damaged property.

The ceiba tree (left above) is called the silk cotton tree. Rare orchids (right top) and armadillos (right bottom) are found in the forests.

PLANTS AND ANIMALS

The warm, wet tropics in Honduras nourish great varieties of plants and animals. Mountain peaks higher than 7,000 feet (2,134 meters) harbor *cloud forests*, jungles of ferns, broadleaf plants, and evergreen trees blanketed in mist. Moist woods contain mosses, wild avocados, and rare orchids. Between the peaks are unusual patches of desert and grassland.

Pine, fir, and oak trees cover large areas below these peaks. Forests of mahogany, silk cotton, Spanish cedar, and rosewood mixed with palm and pine grow in lowland regions. Mangroves line the coasts, while acacias and cactus bloom in the savannas of the northeast.

Honduran forests shelter many common animals. Anteaters, armadillos, deer, raccoons, turkeys, and pumas roam the country.

*Some animals of Honduras
(clockwise from left) are:
the red-eyed tree frog,
the manatee,
and the coati.*

Rarer coatis, sloths, lizards, and species of snakes and rodents
make their homes in the various regions.

Nearer the water are crocodiles, caymans, turtles, manatees,
salamanders, and frogs. Many forms of familiar and unfamiliar
game fish surround the Bay Islands. Lake Yojoa is home to black
bass. The seas house mollusks, snails, lobsters, shrimps, and crabs.
Sea creatures may hold the future for a budding fishing industry.

Bird-watchers find Honduran rain forests a treasure chest. In
the Lancetilla Botanical Garden near Tela you can see most bird
species found in the country. A favorite is the quetzal, a rare bird
with long tail feathers that is found mainly in Central America.
Among other local birds are the black robin, wood hewer,

Interesting birds (left to right) are: a curassow, a quetzal, and a motmot.

clorospinga, motmot, curassow, wild hen, and tanamou. More common hummingbirds, quails, parrots, macaws, vultures, and ducks also live in the tropics.

NATURAL RESOURCES

During different periods of Honduran history, the mountains have been a source of wealth. Gold and silver first attracted Spaniards to Honduran interior highlands centuries ago. Small deposits of lead, zinc, tin, iron, coal, antimony, and silver have encouraged mining through the centuries. Marble, gypsum, and limestone have been extracted from the mountains for building since the time when the Maya roamed western Honduras.

Most electrical energy comes from imported oil and hydroelectric power. An oil refinery in Puerto Cortés processes unrefined foreign oil for Hondurans. Important hydroelectric plants at Río Lindo, El Nispers, and El Cajon give hope of developing Honduras's vast hydroelectric potential. For now, most Hondurans gather wood to heat their homes and cook meals.

The slash-and-burn method of clearing the land for agriculture has destroyed acres of forest.

SAVING THE ENVIRONMENT

Like many countries, Honduras is in danger of losing the very land that supports its people. For decades, large foreign companies have held vast acreage for banana plantations. Contractors have discovered ancient Mayan treasures while building power plants. Rural farmers continue to destroy miles of forests with age-old slash-and-burn agriculture. To clear land for orchards and farms, they burn acres of forest in fires that they often are unable to control. Similarly, oil exploration and logging devastate the tropical forests.

More recently, environmental groups have fought to reverse the damage to forests, plants, and animals. People inside and outside Honduras pressed the Honduran government to safeguard natural resources. These efforts have had mixed results.

Honduras has joined other Central American countries in an effort to preserve their Maya heritage. Government-controlled roads and tourist accommodations attempt to ensure that the country can profit from the past without destroying its treasures.

Other groups pressure companies to take responsibility for replacing and protecting the resources they use. Cultural Survival, a group that helps Indians preserve their land, launched a campaign on behalf of the Tawahka Indians. The Tawahka live on about 1,500 square miles (3,885 square kilometers) of La Mosquitia.

The group encouraged supporters to press the Honduran government to create a reserve on Tawahka homelands. The reserve would give the Tawahka the rights to manage their land without invasion from colonists or corporations. These are only a few of the efforts needed to help Hondurans preserve their future.

Chapter 3

THE MAYAN PAST

THE GREAT MAYAN CIVILIZATION

Three noble Indian civilizations (Aztec, Inca, and Maya) populated the land from Mexico to South America long before Spanish explorers arrived in the Western Hemisphere. For thousands of years, these Indians hunted for food and grew crops such as *maize*, corn, to survive. They created complex societies and built monuments and buildings, some that have lasted until today.

In Central America many Indian nations with common traditions and language formed the Mayan civilization. Maya Indians lived in present-day Honduras, El Salvador, Guatemala, and Mexico. At its height, the Mayan civilization included about three million people.

Maya Indians settled the countryside and established large cities throughout the narrow strip of land connecting North and South America. Archaeologists have discovered remains of ancient Mayan cities more than twenty-five thousand years old. Most claim, however, that an early classic period in Mayan history spanned from A.D. 250 to 900. During this time the Maya constructed great cities, prospered in agriculture, and developed advanced ideas about science and astronomy.

Opposite page: An ancient painted clay statue of a Mayan Indian god

A ball court used for Maya games in Copán

The classic period experienced construction of about two hundred Mayan cities in Mexico, Guatemala, Belize, and parts of El Salvador and Honduras. Four major centers of Mayan civilization were created during this period. One of the most advanced was located on the Copán River in present-day western Honduras. This Mayan city was called Copán.

MAYAN SOCIETY

Mayan society was divided into strata, or ranks, based on family wealth. At the bottom of the social ranks were slaves, who were usually captured in battle. Next were peasant farmers and laborers. Above them were merchants and craftspeople who served the warriors and priests.

For most of the classic period, priests ruled as leaders. They decided who worked the land and how crops were distributed

*A Maya mural shows a settlement near a river
and the daily activities of its inhabitants.*

and traded. Many priests ordered peasants to build grand
pyramids and temples. The remains of these religious buildings
reflect the amount of power priests held over their subjects.

Some historians believe that every Mayan community formed
its own city-state, or government. Each city-state included
thousands of citizens. City-states operated independently, and each
had its own ruler. A ruler's empire extended as far as a person
could walk or travel by canoe in a single day.

Other historians believe that individual city-states formed a
larger confederation, a loosely formed government. Common
beliefs linked these smaller societies into one government. A
complex network of trade routes and canals and the need for
products such as wax, honey, salt, furs, feathers, jade, and cotton
became a uniting bond.

Often city-states fought with one another, whether they had a
common government or not. Toward the end of the classic period

Maya hieroglyphics

conflict increased. A few historians claim that constant fighting among tribes eventually led to the downfall of the Mayan civilization.

MAYAN ACHIEVEMENTS

Archaeologists are just beginning to reveal the wonders of ancient Mayan culture. Recent discoveries have helped them decode the *hieroglyphics*, picture writing, of the Maya people. By studying writings on *stelae*, limestone slabs, and observing remains of buildings and pottery, historians learn how the ancient Maya lived and what they achieved.

Researchers have uncovered parts of pyramids, palaces, temples, and aqueducts built by the Maya. They marvel that such detailed, large structures were built without wheels, metal tools, or pack animals to haul materials. The walls of these ruins display picture

This is the entrance to a Maya tomb.

symbols of daily activities. The Maya developed a complex language and writing system from these symbols. They recorded stories about their leaders, important battles, births, deaths, and other basic facts that were carved into stone for future generations to see.

The greatest source of information about Mayan society comes from tombs. The Maya buried their dead in special buildings close to where they lived. Bodies of family members became part of ritual ceremonies. Mayan families buried possessions with the dead. Within the tombs were brightly colored murals and finely sculpted vases. Tombs also contained stone tools and jade and shell rings, necklaces, pendants, and earrings. Dead royalty and commoners were treated much the same, although royal tombs were larger, more decorated, and filled with richer objects. From these objects archaeologists have learned about daily life.

The Maya developed many farming techniques still used today. One method—now questioned by those who want to protect the environment—is called slash-and-burn. Peasants first cleared the land by felling trees with stone tools and then burning all the bush. They dug holes in the scorched ground with sticks. Corn kernels and bean seeds went into each hole. The long bean vines twisted around the cornstalks as both plants grew. To prevent soil erosion, farmers built stone terraces. The slash-and-burn method depleted the soil of nutrients. Farmers moved frequently because fields needed from four to seven years to become fruitful again.

The Maya were one of the few groups to use calendar time. Their calendar of 365 days divided the year into 18 months. Each month had 20 days and five extra days were added at the end of each year. On the extra days, people fasted and held ceremonies to honor their mythical gods. The Maya believed these days to be unlucky. Their prayer rituals were intended to ward off any disaster. After prayers, they celebrated New Year's Day.

The Maya also discovered the concept of zero, which was central to creating a system of numbers. They were the only New World civilization at the time to express the idea.

The American Paper Institute credits the Maya with inventing an early form of paper, made from the bark of fig trees. Artisans beat and softened the fig bark and treated it with water and lime to remove the sap. Then they flattened the bark until it dried and peeled apart in sheets. The institute claims that the Maya produced the first "concertinalike" books, consisting of pages with hard covers. These and other scientific findings made the Maya one of the most advanced societies of the day.

The hieroglyphic stairway in Copán has sixty-three steps and each stone block has a separate hieroglyph.

MAYA IN HONDURAS

The center of Mayan population and power may have been in what is now Guatemala. But the site of the greatest scientific and artistic achievements was in the regional center of Copán in western Honduras. For example, the longest Mayan hieroglyph, a character used in hieroglyphic writing, comes from Copán.

Copán is thought to be the place where the Maya discovered that the planets rotate around the sun. They traced paths of planets without benefit of telescopes. Early Mayan astronomers were able to predict eclipses of the sun.

Cornfields and forested hills along the Copán River

Many researchers believe that Copán was the most beautiful of all the Mayan cities. Fancy royal pyramids, delicate stone patterns on buildings, and colorful figurines show the splendor of long ago. The city's location on the banks of the Copán River 2,100 feet (640 meters) above sea level and surrounded by forested mountains added to its beauty. Rich soil around the city permitted peasants to grow enough food for all residents in the city. Little wonder that the lovely Copán became home to scientists, priests, and merchants.

The last dated hieroglyph from Copán reads A.D. 800. After that Copán fell into ruin. As Mayan civilization declined, priests, scientists, and rulers vanished.

MAYA DECLINE

When Columbus landed on the Caribbean coast of Honduras, he encountered descendants of the Maya who had created this great civilization. Columbus's ships reached Guanaja, the easternmost island off the coast of Honduras, in July 1502. This was Columbus's fourth voyage to the Western Hemisphere.

A giant canoe with a roof of palm leaves met his party. About fifty Maya Indians were on board. They carried colorful woven garments, pottery, copper, stone tools, and cacao beans for exchange as money. Columbus ordered the boat and its contents seized. Thus began the Spanish conquest of Central America.

By that time, however, the Mayan civilization that had once spread across many countries was in decline. Conflicts among individual Mayan tribes had increased since the classic period. Spaniards used these conflicts to divide and conquer the Indians. After each battle, the Spaniards stepped in to enslave the surviving Indians and occupy the land. The Maya tried to resist Spanish control, but their simple weapons were no match for European guns and horses. Many Maya died in battle or from diseases carried by the Europeans.

Some Maya who lived retained their language and culture despite great violence against them. Descendants of these people live today in the mountains of Guatemala. Many others in Central America gave up their traditional way of life. In Honduras traditional Indian culture did not survive Spanish conquest. Today, however, Hondurans and others around the world are interested in studying the classic Mayan period. They seek to uncover the links between early Mayan contributions to civilization and the way Central Americans live now.

Chapter 4

SPANISH OCCUPATION

FINAL CONQUEST

Twenty years after Columbus's arrival, Spain sent large armies to complete the conquest of Central America. Spain wanted riches such as gold and silver, no matter what the cost to native people who inhabited the land. Spanish armies crushed Indian revolts and established the Kingdom of Guatemala. The kingdom included present-day Guatemala, Nicaragua, Costa Rica, El Salvador, part of Mexico, and Honduras. The administrative capital of the Spanish empire in Central America changed from one to another of three Guatemalan cities, the last being Guatemala City.

INDIAN REBELLIONS

Spanish colonists created settlements in the new land. They dug mines for gold and silver, built plantations to grow crops, and established churches. The settlers expected the Indians to provide labor for these projects. But the Indians claimed the land belonged to their nation. They followed their own customs and ways of

Spaniards led by Cortés occupied the land and angered the Indians enough to cause them to fight.

growing food and lashed out at the Spanish invaders. Frequent battles between the Spaniards and Indians continued throughout the sixteenth century.

Lempira, a Lenca Indian living in Honduras, was outraged by the Spanish occupation of Indian lands. He hated the Spanish plan to enslave the entire Indian population. Lempira organized three thousand followers to fight Spanish control in Central America. For two years Lempira and his soldiers pushed back Spanish armies. From 1537 to 1539 Lempira's warriors seized control of 300 square miles (777 square kilometers) in western Honduras, which earned him the name "Lord of the Mountains."

Lempira's army fought with bows and arrows against Spanish guns. Yet the Indians almost defeated the Spaniards. To end the war, Spanish officers called for peace talks. Lempira believed the Europeans wanted peace and agreed to negotiate, but Spanish soldiers tricked the Mayan leader and ordered him killed. With the native leader dead, the Spanish army easily defeated the Indians in the rebellion that followed. Much later, Hondurans named their currency after Lempira to remind the people how he fought bravely to preserve their freedom.

Indians organized frequent revolts over the next 280 years. Still, Spanish control expanded throughout Central America. The conquerors removed whatever gold and silver they found in the mines and sent it to the Spanish king. Colonists built plantations to grow sugar and plants for dyes used for clothing in Europe. As they settled the land, the Spanish took most of the riches that belonged to the native population.

One of Spain's first plans after defeating the Indians was to create a system of slavery in Central America. The Spanish king granted plantation or mine owners the right to control any Indians who lived where the Spanish settled. Spain sent missionaries to establish churches that "civilized" the Indians. That is, they encouraged the Indians to adopt Spanish customs. That way, the Spaniards believed, Indians would be more willing to obey.

Indian slaves proved too costly to feed, clothe, and house. After a time, Spain adopted a new policy. Spanish landlords or mine owners required Indians to guarantee so many hours of work each week. One or two days a week Indians worked for their landlord; the rest of the time they worked and cared for themselves.

This plan eventually led to a system of paid wages instead of forced labor. But Indians were required to borrow money from landowners to pay for food or to rent small plots of land to grow their own food. This newer arrangement kept Indians indebted to their wealthy landlords. Spanish colonists and their descendants continued to abuse the Indians and their land.

Some Hondurans are descended from African slaves.

Slavery, forced labor, and disease contributed to the death of thousands of Indians during the colonial period. One estimate claimed that 85 percent of the Indian population died of war or disease brought by the Spaniards between 1524 and 1650. By the 1980s only forty-three thousand descendants of Indians remained in Honduras.

The Spaniards also brought a small number of African slaves to Honduras during the sixteenth century. By 1545 almost two thousand slaves worked the fields and mines or were personal servants. Their descendants form 2 percent of the Honduran population today.

COLONIAL ECONOMY

The Spaniards first came to the New World expecting to find gold and silver. For a short time, they discovered isolated deposits throughout Central America. The biggest riches were in the Honduran region. By 1540 explorers had located major gold

*When the Spaniards saw the Indians' gold objects,
they wanted to find the source of the gold.*

deposits at Gracias in western Honduras and along the Guaypo River in the eastern province of Olancho. Gracias soon became the capital of colonial Spain, but gold supplies quickly dwindled. The Spaniards moved their colonial capital to Panama and then to Guatemala, where it remained until Central American independence.

In 1578 silver deposits were discovered in the mountains where Tegucigalpa is today. Colonial governors established two separate provinces near the silver mines. One centered around Tegucigalpa, and the other began some thirty miles (forty-eight kilometers) away in what became Comayagua. Later, Honduran leaders from these two provinces competed with each other for control of the Honduran government.

By the middle of the sixteenth century, most mining ended in Honduras. Greedy colonists had taken all the gold and silver from the mines. The colonists then looked for different activities to gain riches for Spain, but most proved unsuccessful. Cattle raising and the making of leather and other products from cattle were short-lived. Plantation owners grew plants such as indigo and cochineal for dyes, herbs such as balsam and sarsaparilla for medicines, and cacao.

In each case, other countries grew and sold better, cheaper crops and goods. By the eighteenth century, the local economy depended on agricultural subsistence. This meant that most people grew only those crops they needed to survive and that few products earned money from trade overseas.

A major barrier to economic success was the rugged Honduran countryside. The mountains that divided the country made it difficult to expand farming operations and caused problems with travel and communication. The lack of good ports limited contact with the outside world. As a result, Spain saw little reason to invest in education or cultural activities. Honduras became a forgotten colony.

Conflict developed among big landowners, who vied for whatever limited power there was to gain. Indians continued to be treated poorly and refused to cooperate whenever they could. Difficult conditions kept the region economically and politically weak, compared with other Spanish settlements.

CENTRAL AMERICAN INDEPENDENCE

Toward the close of the eighteenth century, new conflicts arose. Landowners clashed with the Spanish government. Landowners were prohibited from selling farm goods to any other country except Spain. They claimed they lost opportunities for much-needed trade and profits. Spain, the landowners agreed, held too much control over the Central American economy.

Criollos, people of Spanish background who were born in the colonies, and *ladinos* or *mestizos*, people of mixed Spanish and Indian backgrounds, raised their voices against Spanish economic and political control. Indians joined these protests with organized revolts against Spanish rule.

Rising protest and violence throughout Central America led Mexico to announce its independence from Spain in 1821. On September 21, 1821, a group in Guatemala City declared all of Central America independent.

Hondurans from Comayagua wanted to become part of Mexico. Those from Tegucigalpa opposed this idea. A brief war broke out between leaders of the two cities. Conflict between different Mexican leaders added to the confusion.

UNITED PROVINCES OF CENTRAL AMERICA

By 1823 Central Americans formed their own independent government without Mexico. A confederation, an organization of Central American states, was created and called the United Provinces of Central America. Within a year, the Central Americans wrote a constitution for the confederation. The constitution created a fairly strong government but allowed for each participating state (Costa Rica, El Salvador, Guatemala, Honduras, and Nicaragua) to rule itself independently.

The constitution of 1824 represented many ideas of a group known as liberals. They supported limits on the power and privileges of the Catholic Church. They favored an end to slavery, less taxes on trade, public education, and an increase in trade by building ports and roads. Moreover, liberals believed in a single Central American government—but one that guaranteed freedom for each state.

The opposing group, the conservatives, championed the political and economic policies of Spanish colonialism. They supported economic benefits for the Catholic Church and preferred maintaining close trade ties with Spain rather than expanding trade worldwide. Conservatives also promised to keep Indians in a lowly position. Moreover, they favored control from a central government in Guatemala City that was similar to the government that existed under Spanish rule.

HONDURAN INDEPENDENCE

Conflict and open violence between liberals and conservatives interfered with governing the United Provinces. Liberals controlled the government from 1823 to 1825, and conservatives gained power in 1826. President Manuel Arce, a former liberal who became a conservative, sent armies into Honduras in 1826 to crush a liberal revolt. One year later, Francisco Morazán, a Honduran soldier and son of criollo parents, led an army that captured the United Provinces government for the liberals.

For the next thirteen years Morazán unsuccessfully struggled to keep Central America united. He opened land and trade to foreign countries, which angered Spanish landowners. He offended the church by reducing its power, and he enraged the Indians because he tried to end the collective ownership of Indian lands that was part of their tradition.

The Central American economy suffered from Morazán's failed policies. Foreign control and bad loans from British bankers weakened the region. Morazán and his followers attempted to establish schools, a central government, and courts similar to those in northern Europe and the United States. These efforts to make Central America more modern and open also failed. Morazán fought twenty-one battles from 1827 until 1839. His last struggle marked the end of the United Provinces of Central America.

After years of unrest, José Rafael Carrera, a Guatemalan ladino leader with close ties to the Indian community, led a revolt against the United Provinces. Honduras declared its independence on October 26, 1838. The following January, Honduran leaders adopted the country's first constitution. By the end of 1839, Costa Rica, Honduras, Guatemala, and Nicaragua had separated from the confederation. The united government of Central America was history.

A statue of Francisco Morazán stands in Tegucigalpa.

Morazán fled to Peru. Two years later his followers attacked the government of Costa Rica in a hopeless bid to restore unity. After this battle, Morazán was finally overthrown, captured, and killed.

With Morazán's death the dream of a united Central America also died. Many Central Americans who prefer a combined region regard him as the George Washington of Central America. Of the five countries that developed, Honduras would become the poorest. All that survived for Hondurans was the memory of their military and political hero of the federation, Francisco Morazán.

Chapter 5

INDEPENDENT

HONDURAS

The new Honduran government remained weak and divided after the breakup of the United Provinces of Central America. Geography separated large landowners. They controlled their regions but had little contact with the powerless national government. Each armed landowner battled to take over greater regions and national leadership. For the next seventy-five years, sixty-four different governments ruled Honduras.

Constantly changing governments left Honduras open to foreign intervention. Exiles from neighboring El Salvador, Guatemala, and Nicaragua launched attacks from inside Honduran borders to topple their governments. British and United States agents plotted to get rich at Honduras's expense. Agents prodded the Honduran government to borrow large sums of money to invest in mines and other questionable programs.

Hondurans dabbled in more mining, the cattle industry, and crops for export. None of these industries brought sizable fortunes into the country. Projects to build roads, ports, and railroads rarely reached completion, and most Hondurans traveled along dirt mule trails, as regions were isolated from each other.

During the mid-1800s, Britain pressed Honduras to pay its

debts, even those for unfinished projects. The British government seized part of the Mosquito Coast, Bay Islands, and Tigre Island, while the British navy occupied the port at Trujillo.

The United States moved to protect its own growing interests in Central America by threatening the British in Honduras. The British troops refused to leave, however. Honduras continued to owe money to foreign bankers, and foreigners continued to take part in the Honduran government.

Without money, the Honduran government offered little education and poor health care services to the people. By the late 1800s, Honduras was without a national newspaper and had built only one library, one university, and scattered primary schools. Cities, including Tegucigalpa, lacked water systems, and city residents had to hand-carry water from the river. Sewage disposal was a constant problem without running water. Because there was no garbage collection, coastal dwellers threw waste into the sea, while inland residents collected and burned piles of garbage. Awful living conditions caused widespread disease. In 1892 an outbreak of yellow fever was so severe businesses closed for months.

Other Central American countries attracted investors with crops, such as coffee, to export. Large sums of money flowed into these countries, creating small groups of wealthy and powerful citizens. Nineteenth-century Honduras never experienced similar booms. Hondurans remained extremely poor compared to their neighbors.

BANANA COMPANIES

Central American banana traders came to Honduras during the late nineteenth century. At first, they created a banana trade to

Bananas are boxed (left) and then loaded onto train cars (right) for shipment to the port.

help railroads prosper in neighboring countries. In the 1890s the Honduran government contracted with Britain to complete a railroad from Puerto Cortés to San Pedro Sula.

The Vaccaro brothers of New Orleans, Louisiana, shipped the first boatload of bananas from Honduras to New Orleans in 1899. They found that banana sales earned huge profits in the United States. Thereafter, they and other merchants expanded Honduran banana exports.

American companies bought huge tracts of land in Honduras, hired thousands of workers, and began producing bananas on a bigger scale. Three large companies and several smaller traders dominated the Honduran banana business. The Vaccaro brothers started Standard Fruit in 1904, and Sam "the banana man" Zemurray began the Cuyamel Company in 1911. By then bananas accounted for 66 percent of Honduran exports.

The largest banana company in Honduras, however, was United Fruit. In 1929 United Fruit bought out Zemurray and made him

Workers' housing on a banana plantation near San Pedro Sula

president of the combined company. When Zemurray retired in 1950, United Fruit employed eighty-two thousand workers in many South and Central American countries.

Banana merchants held a great deal of power in Honduras, beyond trade. Foreign business people influenced those who ran for office and supported laws favoring the banana industry. Companies plotted to gain tax breaks and grants for building wharfs, roads, and railroads to transport bananas.

In return, banana companies constructed housing for workers and provided them with basic services. With these benefits, however, came low pay. Workers lived in crowded quarters. They bought goods from stores owned by the company and, because wages were so low, were unable to get out of debt. A main transportation route now carried goods from Tegucigalpa to the Pacific coast, but the railroads brought only bananas from the fields to ports. Hondurans still walked from town to town.

The banana industry never created the small wealthy group of citizens in Honduras that such industries created in other Central American countries. Banana companies paid few or no taxes, and they took their profits out of the country. The Honduran dream of developing a valuable product to sell worldwide did little to benefit the country's economy and people.

THE CARIAS DICTATORSHIP

Government unrest continued into the twentieth century. Honduras averaged one president per year. The two parties, liberal and conservative, that existed throughout Central America were in Honduras as well. Their weak leaders vied for control of the continually changing government.

The modern Liberal Party was started in 1891, and the modern conservative party, called the National Party, was founded in 1927. The parties disagreed on a number of policies. Both relied on the military to enforce laws, however, and both were influenced by the United States government and banana companies.

By 1930 Honduras was the world's leading banana producer. One-third of the world's bananas came from Honduras. United Fruit remained the most important banana company. Still, the people remained as poor, uneducated, and isolated in rural communities as before. Along with foreign control of the economy, transportation persisted as a significant roadblock to making economic and political gains in Honduras.

Then the world depression began. Economic problems worsened as purchases of bananas and all other goods declined. Thousands of workers lost their jobs, and those who still had jobs received smaller paychecks. Worker protests erupted in response to terrible conditions.

General Tiburcio Carías Andino (left) and President Manuel Gálvez (right)

In 1932 National Party member General Tiburcio Carías Andino was elected president. To control unrest, Carías ended popular elections. He ordered the army to silence opponents and ruled as head of the military until 1948.

During his years in power, Carías imprisoned enemies, banned newspapers, and allowed his soldiers to shoot protesters. He appointed members of the National Party to lead armies in different parts of the country.

Carías usually obeyed orders from the United Fruit Company. In 1948, however, enemies and pressure from the United States forced Carías out of office. Honduras held its first free election in sixteen years.

1954 WORKER STRIKE

The close of World War II brought many changes to Honduras. Manuel Gálvez replaced Carías. His government created a national bank, spent money to build some roads and other public projects, and gave government loans to large farmers to persuade them to grow cotton, sugar, and coffee and to raise cattle. Hondurans started producing crops other than bananas for the first time in decades.

A few factories and businesses opened to turn crops into products for sale. A small middle class of doctors, lawyers, and business people emerged. Greater numbers of Hondurans worked in factories and on plantations.

The military, however, became more powerful in the government. The United States sent advisers to upgrade the army. The United States government increased its involvement in the political and economic life of the country.

In 1954 workers at the railroad owned by United Fruit Company called a strike. They wanted higher wages, better working conditions, and the right to join a union of their choice. The strike spread to Standard Fruit, other banana plantations, and dock workers. Within a month almost thirty thousand Hondurans left their jobs. The nation's banana industry came to a standstill. Union representatives from the United States offered to help the companies and workers resolve their differences.

The outcome of the landmark banana strike was mixed. United Fruit and the Honduran government agreed to recognize the union. United Fruit was one of the last companies in Central America to give workers the right to join unions. Workers also gained increases in their low wages.

Over the years, however, the fruit company reduced the number of workers it employed. United Fruit bought more machinery to pick bananas and haul them to market. The strong leaders in the struggle for worker's rights were forced from union positions and lost their jobs on plantations, railroads, and docks. The remaining union leaders were less likely to challenge company bosses. Still, Honduras developed a strong labor movement in 1954 that continues to defend worker rights today.

Later, the banana companies sold their plantations and bought bananas from Honduran producers. These producers dealt with the angry workers. The major banana companies only transported the bananas from Honduras and sold them around the world.

PEASANT REVOLT

Rural peasants also demanded rights. Foreign banana companies and a small number of wealthy Hondurans owned the best farmland. Poor farmers were left with rocky land in central Honduras.

Some land reforms occurred during the 1960s and 1970s when small parcels of land were given to peasants. New laws prohibited farmland from going unused. In a few areas land holdings of more than 1,235 acres (500 hectares) were divided among local peasants. About 12 percent of rural families were allowed to occupy land owned by the government. Peasants banded together in farm cooperatives. Cooperatives permitted individual peasants to share production and services at a lower cost.

Reform laws helped some peasants. However, these laws required more land and resources than were available to provide for the large numbers of poor peasants who needed both to grow food for themselves and earn a decent living. As peasants continued to push for more changes, the government moved to quiet protesters by putting them in jail. Protests spread throughout the countryside.

Despite reform efforts, 90 percent of Hondurans earned less than 50 percent of the nation's income in 1980. Seven international corporations controlled 80 percent of the Honduran economy. These companies included United Brands and Castle & Cooke, descendants of the old banana companies. Five percent of the people controlled more than 50 percent of the land. Farm exports, such as bananas and sugar, increased fivefold between 1960 and 1970, yet food production during this time decreased by 20 percent.

SOCCER WAR

The banana companies brought thousands of people from El Salvador to work on Honduran plantations over the years. During the 1960s several thousand more Salvadorans migrated to Honduras seeking farmland. Hondurans resented Salvadorans who occupied scarce land.

About the same time, Honduras joined its neighbors in the Central American Common Market (CACM) to establish additional markets for goods. CACM permitted El Salvador and Guatemala to gain trade advantages with Honduras. The Honduran people disliked any foreign traders, especially Salvadorans, making money at their expense.

In the spring of 1969 tensions mounted. Honduras expelled several Salvadoran families. Soon after, Salvadoran newspapers charged that Hondurans had poisoned Salvadoran soccer players at a match in Tegucigalpa. Salvadorans countered with an attack on Honduran players at a match in San Salvador. The Honduran government deported thousands more Salvadorans. The Salvadoran army responded by invading Honduras. A battle

An OAS official interviews a Salvadoran (left).
Some of the destruction from the Soccer War (right).

raged for one hundred hours. The Organization of American States (OAS) stepped in to end the fighting just as Honduras neared defeat.

After the war Honduran generals demanded that the military receive more money and training. They refused to be embarrassed by the Salvadoran army again. The result was that the military assumed a larger role in Honduran political life during the 1970s.

The short Soccer War led to a breakdown of the CACM. Hostilities between Honduras and El Salvador continued into the 1980s. Constant bitterness made it difficult for the United States to enlist Honduran support to bolster the Salvadoran military government.

CENTRAL AMERICAN WARS

The United States expanded interests in Central America during the 1980s. United States President Ronald Reagan charged that the

Left: Nicaraguan soldiers at their camp in Honduras. Right: Honduran soldiers

Nicaraguan government took orders from the Soviet Union and was a threat to the region. He organized a small army of Nicaraguans to fight their government.

President Reagan also backed the wealthy coffee growers and military-run government of El Salvador. He provided millions of dollars in military aid to help El Salvador silence the protests of the peasant population against poor living and working conditions.

Honduras became important in these conflicts because both countries were neighbors. The United States bribed Honduran military leaders to support U.S. policies against the Nicaraguan government and against protesters fighting the Salvadoran government. As the wars dragged on, Honduras received large amounts of U.S. military aid to protect its borders from invasion.

The U.S. army built airfields and military bases across Honduras. They stationed troops in Honduras and ran frequent military exercises with the Honduran army. United States soldiers trained Salvadoran troops at bases in Honduras. They allowed Nicaraguan fighters to establish bases along the Nicaragua-Honduras border. By 1987 about twenty thousand Nicaraguan soldiers lived in Honduras in camps paid for by the United States. The camps became bases for soldiers to attack sites within Nicaragua.

Some Honduran military officers and business and government people liked the attention and money Honduras received from the United States. They hoped the new importance of their country to the United States would create a flow of dollars and products to help Honduras develop economically.

Others, however, worried that Honduras would become one large military base and that the traditional economy and way of life in Honduras would end. Hondurans along the Nicaraguan border protested against Nicaraguans who occupied lands where the Hondurans grew coffee. They feared that Honduras would be drawn into a large Central American war. These fears helped pressure the United States to allow Central America nations to negotiate an end to the violent conflicts that engulfed the region. Even with greater calm, the region has remained unstable and most people still are poor.

Political parties and small peasant groups formed to protest government and economic policies. Rural peasants occupied unused land and protested the lack of food and farmland. Outsiders have continued to dominate the economy and the government. Little has changed since the early 1800s, when Honduras fought for the United Provinces of Central America in the hope of forming a peaceful and prosperous government in the region.

Chapter 6

HONDURAS TODAY

Honduras is the poorest, least-developed country in Central America. Only about 10 percent of the workforce have secure jobs. Hondurans who have jobs earn about $800 per year. Peasant farmers sometimes earn less than $70 a year.

Currently, most workers are facing a decline in income as prices for everyday goods rise. Decreased income means that fewer Hondurans eat the foods they need to stay healthy. Hard times force many rural Hondurans to seek jobs in cities.

Honduras's hope for reducing poverty lies in the government's willingness to set limits on foreign investors. The government frequently issues new money for projects to modernize and expand the Honduran economy. Foreign investors have been in the best position to take advantage of these grants and loans. Therefore, most of the funds end up in programs that provide profits for foreign bank accounts.

AGRICULTURE

Agriculture supplies the largest share of Honduras's total employment, earnings, and production. A majority of Hondurans live in rural areas and engage in agricultural work. Only 50

Opposite page: Although Honduras is a poor country, the government is trying to modernize and expand the economy.

Foreign companies still control the banana plantations.

percent of these people own land, however, and the land usually covers less than five acres (two hectares).

A small number of Hondurans run large farms. The major agricultural producers continue to be foreign companies that control vast banana plantations. Only 20 percent of Honduran land in valleys and coastal plains is fertile. Of that land, the government and two international companies, United Brands and Castle & Cooke, own 60 percent.

Bananas are the number-one crop produced in Honduras and exported to the United States and Europe. Honduras remains one

Coffee beans must be specially packed before they are shipped for processing.

of the largest suppliers of bananas, or "yellow gold," in the
world. United Brands exports more than 33 percent of the
bananas through its Tela Railroad division, which sells the
Chiquita brand.

In 1992 the government approved laws to expand banana
investments. Newly farmed land received three-year tax breaks.
The National Banana Council was formed to boost banana
production and exports.

Besides bananas, Honduras produces coffee. Most coffee
growers are small or mid-sized landholding farmers. They employ
large numbers of Hondurans to supply coffee for export. Without
technical assistance, however, Honduran coffee farms produce
fewer crops at greater cost than other coffee-producing countries.
Although coffee accounts for 20 percent of exports, it has never
gained the same importance as bananas.

Above: Unloading a catch of fish
Right: Processing lobster tails for export

Beef production decreased during the 1980s, but sales rose during the early 1990s. Ranchers raise cattle by nontechnical methods, and the result is low output. They rely on rain and natural pastures rather than more advanced techniques. More than 25 percent of Honduras's fertile land is used for raising cattle. Many Hondurans believe the scarce land could be used more wisely, such as for crops to feed rural peasants.

Fishing promises to become a profitable industry. The greatest export earnings come from shrimp and lobsters. Shrimp exports jumped from $19 million in 1988 to almost $72 million in 1991. Shrimp farming occurs mainly in the Gulf of Fonseca and on the North Coast. Some small-scale shrimp farmers exist. Money for larger fisheries with advanced technology comes from other countries, such as the United States, Taiwan, and Ecuador.

During the 1980s the Honduran government and investors

began producing crops such as pineapples, melons, spices, cucumbers, and flowers. None of these contributed much to the nation's economy. Food shortages developed as Honduras became deeper in debt to foreign bankers.

According to the World Health Organization, 75 percent of the Honduran people lack the proper vitamins for good health. To ease hunger and restore health, the United States sent large amounts of food aid to Honduras during the 1980s. Wheat imports under food-aid programs provided cheaper grains than corn, a staple in Honduran diets. Hondurans changed their eating habits to include wheat and breads, which deepened dependence on the United States. Problems developed as U.S. interests, including military and food aid, in Central America declined.

MANUFACTURING

Manufacturing accounts for only 16 percent of the Honduran economy and about 9 percent of the workforce. Except for clothing, most products are for sale locally. Factories process food, beverages, tobacco, clothing, and footwear. Farm-related industries include meatpacking, sugar mills, furniture factories, and paper plants.

More than 50 percent of the manufacturing companies are actually family-owned craft shops that employ fewer than ten people. The few wealthy Hondurans or foreign corporations own the nation's larger, more modern factories. Castle & Cooke, a major banana company, makes plastic goods, metal, paper products, cement, and soap. United Brands, Castle's chief banana company rival, produces cooking oils, rubber, and plastic products.

Some modern plants include the Coca-Cola bottling plant in San Pedro Sula and a factory that produces machete blades (inset).

Considerable industrial growth comes from *maquiladoras*. These are government-sponsored factories built by local developers but leased to foreign companies. Maquiladoras are free of government controls. Benefits to the companies are cheap rents, low-wage employees, and nearness to U.S. markets. Without government barriers, foreign companies also save on import, export, and local sales taxes.

Many companies export their machinery and raw materials to Honduras, where local workforces assemble products to be exported for sale in foreign markets. By 1992 several U.S. companies were lured to Honduras by low wages and tax-free bonuses. More than 20 percent of softballs batted in the world were stitched together in Honduras by women working for the Tennessee-based Worth Sports Company. The greatest number of investors, however, came from Korea. Smaller maquiladoras were rented by companies from Singapore, Hong Kong, and Taiwan. Asian-rented companies assembled bicycles, motorcycles, clothing, electronics, and automobiles for shipment worldwide.

Economists question the value of maquiladoras. Companies tend to stay a few years and leave. Even though they provide jobs, most profits from maquiladoras flow out of Honduras. Workers complain of poor and unsafe working conditions and meager wages, but government leaders follow the wishes of foreign companies and are unable to regulate actions by foreign business people.

MINING AND FORESTRY

Government plans for the 1990s included developing mining, oil, and forestry industries. Pine trees cover more than 50 percent of Honduras, but lumber has been a largely untapped resource. Inadequate roads and ports have kept wood exports low. Scattered sawmills process lumber for making furniture, paper, and other wood products. Several U.S. companies manufacture furniture from Honduran lumber.

Honduras also contracted with the United States' Cambria True Oil Company and Venezuela's Maraven to explore La Mosquitia. Texaco (U.S.-based) already runs the nation's single petroleum refinery in Puerto Cortés. The company agreed to further exploration in La Mosquitia as well.

Government officials backed laws that would encourage foreign investors to develop mining. They allotted funds for geological

The first time the National Congress was photographed in session was in 1941, when Honduras declared war on Germany and Italy.

surveys to uncover hidden reserves of zinc, tin, gold, silver, lead, iron, copper, and coal. So far, dreams of huge deposits are part of the hope for an improved Honduran economy. Despite these efforts, Honduras will probably remain mainly an agricultural country for many decades to come.

GOVERNMENT

The Constitutional Assembly of 1980 created the current Honduran constitution, the fourteenth since independence in 1838. Under the constitution, a president leads the government. The president controls the legislative and judicial branches of government and is elected every four years.

The country is divided into eighteen political divisions called *departments*. A major source of power comes from the president's authority to appoint a cabinet and the nation's eighteen department governors. The president also selects people to fill all public posts. In 1984 the number of public employees climbed to a high of seventy thousand.

One hundred twenty-eight representatives make up the National Congress. Representatives are elected every four years. Historically, the Congress agrees with whatever the president decides.

Representatives choose a nine-member Supreme Court. The court's job is to solve problems involving the constitution. The court changes with each new government. This arrangement limits the court's freedom to make its decisions justly, without influence from other branches of government and pressure groups.

Local government is run by 289 community representatives and the National Election Board. The board takes charge of local elections. By law, every Honduran must vote. The only exceptions are soldiers on active military duty, who are not allowed to vote.

The president is the only official elected by popular vote. Congress and local leaders are determined by political party slates or population figures in a given area. Vote cheating is common with each election.

Labor unions and smaller parties oppose laws about political representation because they are too limiting. They call for fairer selection procedures and more open elections. They seek a government that supports their rights to own land, work for decent wages, and earn enough to feed their families.

Pupils from a one-room school in rural Honduras are tickled to be photographed.

Chapter 7

THE PEOPLE
AND THEIR CULTURE

MESTIZOS

At the time of Spanish conquest, between 800,000 and 1.4 million Amerindians lived in Honduras. Spanish slave trade, massacres, diseases, and intermarriage ravaged the native population. Today less than 10 percent of the people claim Indian ancestry. The majority of Hondurans are mestizos. The rest of the population consists of small groups of African-Hondurans, Arabs, and Europeans.

Mestizos live throughout the country and follow many patterns set by Spanish colonists. Mestizos are mainly Catholic, and they speak Spanish, the nation's official language. Traders in port cities speak some English for international business.

AMERINDIANS

Two broad Amerindian groups remain in Honduras. Those who settled farm communities in the west descended from the Maya. They include fifty thousand Lenca, who bravely fought Spanish conquest, and smaller numbers of Chorti from Copán, Chorotega,

Miskito women

and Pipil. The Spanish resettled many of these groups into villages modeled after Spanish towns. Spaniards forced the Indians to farm their plantations, worship in the Catholic Church, and speak Spanish.

The Lenca and Chorti retained many customs from their elders, and the Pipil kept their Nahuatl language. Chorti men can be seen wearing white shirts and trousers like those of their Indian ancestors from Mexico. Lenca women dress in long skirts and short blouses similar to those worn by Spanish women in colonial days. Lenca men and women plant their communal land with corn, squash, and beans. They farm with digging sticks and carry loads on their backs, rather than use plows and pack animals. They craft pottery and baskets with patterns from long ago.

The forest Indians of northeastern Honduras are the other major native group. Within this group, Miskitos and Sumos live in isolated communities much like their ancestors did. They hunt, fish, and grow root crops by the slash-and-burn method. When

Black Caribs on the island of Roatán perform a ceremonial dance.

the soil is depleted, they move to other rain forest settlements. Most still speak a form of Miskito language but practice Christianity according to the Moravian Church. Missionaries translated the Moravian Bible and hymns into the Miskito language during the mid-nineteenth century. Free medical care and the flood of missionaries that followed strengthened the religion among the Miskito.

GARÍFUNA AND ARABS

Garífuna, or Black Caribs, mainly inhabit the northern coast of Honduras near Trujillo and La Ceiba. Others live on the island of Roatán in the settlement of Punta Gorda. The Garífuna originated from African slaves and Carib Indians who lived on the Caribbean island of St. Vincent. British rulers forced unruly Caribs to move to Roatán, where they remained. There they built huts on stilts and became expert sailors, boatbuilders, and fishers.

Modern Black Caribs combine customs from their African origins with British West Indian traditions. They speak an Arawak Indian language as well as Spanish and English. They blend formal Catholic ceremonies with African practices.

Other ethnic groups have come and gone throughout Honduran history. British pirates and merchants were periodically shipwrecked and stayed on the Bay Islands. Development of foreign-owned businesses brought skilled laborers and businesses. One group to come during the early twentieth century was the Lebanese. More arrived after battles between Israel and Lebanon. Hondurans call these and other Arab-speaking Christian immigrants from the Middle East *Turkos* or *Arabes*.

Recent conflicts in Nicaragua, Guatemala, and El Salvador resulted in a rush of more than thirty-five thousand immigrants into Honduras. Government and foreign relief agencies set up refugee camps along Honduran borders. For now, foreign groups outside Honduras and the United States government have provided for the immigrants.

WOMEN AND FAMILIES

Men and women in Honduras hold traditional views found in most Central American countries. Families are strong and children valued. Family ties determine jobs, promotions, and marriages, particularly in the city.

Yet few men and women marry, especially in rural areas. This is due in part to the cost of a wedding and shortage of priests. Some men who don't marry move from household to household, starting new families in each. Married and single women are responsible for the children and household, whether they work

A mother and her children

outside the home or not. Almost half the households in Honduras are headed by women.

Women have few rights under Honduran law. Widows of landowners find that family land goes to their sons over age sixteen, unless their husbands had arranged differently. Men, however, are free to come and go without question and inherit family wealth. Fathers usually make family decisions unopposed. Outside the home most men take the best jobs and decide what roles are fit for their women.

Caring for six to ten children alone forced Honduran women to join together. Honduras has one of the stronger women's movements in Central America. Organizing for rights goes back to the 1920s and the first women's group, Women's Culture Society. The group was founded by Visitacíon Padilla to gain rights for families of banana and mine workers. Women's groups fought successfully for suffrage (the right to vote) in 1954, although men and women still vote in separate locations. They also helped pass the 1984 Family Code, the country's first step toward giving rights to children in homes with single mothers.

Many modern women's groups started in local Catholic churches as mothers' clubs. The groups discussed common problems, distributed food to underfed children, and planted vegetable gardens. As attendance grew, the clubs united. Leaders traveled into other rural areas to organize more mothers' clubs. Women talked about the most serious community problems and how to solve them.

Through the success of these groups, some women assumed unofficial leadership roles within their communities. People came to them for counseling. Lay women ran Sunday Bible services. Women still kept their traditional values, so the men supported them as a way of passing on these traditions.

EDUCATION

Before the 1950s education in Honduras was mainly for the wealthy. Schools cost money, and so did books, uniforms, and supplies that most people could not afford. The government first established the idea of public education in 1957 under President Ramón Villeda Morales. He built schools and pushed for changes in the country's constitution.

Today the constitution still guarantees education for children between seven and twelve years old. But few children benefit from the law. Honduras has a serious shortage of teachers and schools. Only 19 percent of the national budget goes to education. Paying back debts to other countries is allotted 30 percent, and another large portion of the nation's money goes to the military and public services such as roads and communication.

An elementary school in the mountains

Some areas offer education through third grade only. Students who wish to continue must leave home to attend school. About 33 percent of Hondurans never receive formal schooling. Frequent illness causes some children to miss classes. The parents of others keep them home to help earn money for food. Many more families, however, find that schools are too few and too far from their villages.

Children who attend school often experience substandard education. Teachers obtain outdated and inferior training in the Honduran school system and lack the skills to pass information on to their students. Classwork concentrates on language and Honduran history and government. Few children get enough reading and writing to better themselves, and seven of ten children drop out of school by sixth grade. Consequently, about 44 percent of Honduran adults cannot read or write.

Another problem is low pay—if pay comes regularly at all. Some teachers earn food instead of wages as part of food-for-work programs. They teach with limited materials in run-down buildings.

Children from wealthier families in the city fare much better. They go to private schools, some run by the Catholic Church, that provide a broader education. Besides the basics of reading, writing, and mathematics, students learn English. They are more prepared to take jobs that help better their family's privileged lifestyle.

Primary school lasts for six years. Those who move into secondary school follow one of two tracks: vocational education or preparation for higher education. Although numbers are rising, only 30 percent of first-grade students last until secondary school. Of those, only 8 percent reach postsecondary schools.

The only public university is the National Autonomous University of Honduras (UNAH). It began in 1847 in Tegucigalpa. More than thirty thousand students attend campuses at this location and in San Pedro Sula and La Ceiba. Two other schools prepare students to govern Honduras: Francisco Morazán Military Academy and the Pan American Agricultural School. The Pan American Agricultural School was founded in El Zamorano in 1942 by the United Fruit Company. The school draws students from throughout Central America.

The United States Agency for International Development (AID) funds one of three additional private universities. The curriculum at the University of San Pedro Sula emphasizes skills needed to improve Honduras's place in the international business world. Some argue that the United States created the institution to support its interests and counter anti-U.S. teachings at the national university.

Volunteers travel to villages teaching dental hygiene.

HEALTH CARE

In 1992 the Pan American Health Organization conducted a study of health care among its member nations. Results confirmed that the quality and availability of Honduran health services was among the worst in the Western Hemisphere. Overwhelming poverty contributed to about thirty-five children dying each day. The saddest news is that most of these deaths were from diseases that could have been prevented if Honduras had had the resources.

The constitution provides for national health care and social security. But medical services reach only the 11 percent of the population who can afford the high cost of doctors, drugs, and transportation to medical centers.

The government has constructed rural health clinics. However, most are vacant huts without doctors, medicine, or equipment.

Waste is dumped without regard for proper sanitation.

The majority of the population faces disease from unsanitary water, inefficient waste removal, and difficulties reaching treatment. Such conditions contribute to Honduras's having one of the highest infant death rates (seventy per one thousand) in Latin America. The average life expectancy is sixty-two years, compared with seventy-four in the United States and France.

One major concern is malnutrition. In the countryside almost 77 percent of the population lack money to buy proper food for nourishment. Poor diet leaves Hondurans open to diseases, vitamin deficiencies, and infections, including those that attack individuals already weakened by AIDS (acquired immune deficiency syndrome). Many poor Hondurans who survive childhood grow into sickly adults. When in poor health adults are unable to work at their best, thereby contributing to the cycle of poverty.

A Catholic youngster like this girl makes her first communion when she is about seven years old.

RELIGION

Most modern Hondurans are Roman Catholics. Catholicism is the oldest and strongest religion in the country. Catholic missionaries arrived with the Spanish conquerors in 1521. The Spanish built cathedrals in town squares and claimed the country for their church. Indians who already followed an organized religion merely adapted Catholic traditions to their own. Instead of worshiping nature and idols, Indians honored Catholic saints. Churches rather than caves and monuments became places of worship.

Today Catholic children are baptized at a few months of age and families attend services. Villages hold fiestas for local saints. Older Hondurans pray constantly that their hard lives will get better.

Black Caribs who are Catholic follow many customs from their African origins. On Christmas Day and New Year's Day men wearing masks dance the traditional *yunkunu*. Similar dances and mass displays accompany funerals. Caribs believe the dead play an important role for the living.

For all its history and customs, however, the Catholic Church is not especially strong in Honduras. The church never gained the wealth and power it holds in other Central American countries. Moreover, the church has difficulty attracting priests. A large number of priests and nuns in Honduras are from foreign countries. In 1989 only 70 priests out of 292 were natives.

Rural Hondurans distrust foreigners, who have little understanding of their problems. Traditionally, local churches backed charity programs but never confronted the real community issues of education, hunger, and poverty. More recently, some parishes have organized campesino groups to tackle social concerns. Reading programs developed as a result of trying to teach church beliefs. Other groups emphasized technical assistance or acquiring land for the landless. Some priests and nuns ally with the government and the wealthy. They condemn any extreme action on behalf of the poor. Others, however, support change at any cost, even at the cost of their lives.

Various Protestant groups are a fast-growing minority in Honduras. Evangelicals, many funded from the United States, sponsor social service programs to attract members. Some groups send used clothing, toys, medicine, and vitamins. Volunteer teams in La Mosquitia have built churches and led local battles with government and employers. In exchange, these churches spread their beliefs, threatening Catholicism. In 1988, 12 percent of Hondurans claimed to be Protestants.

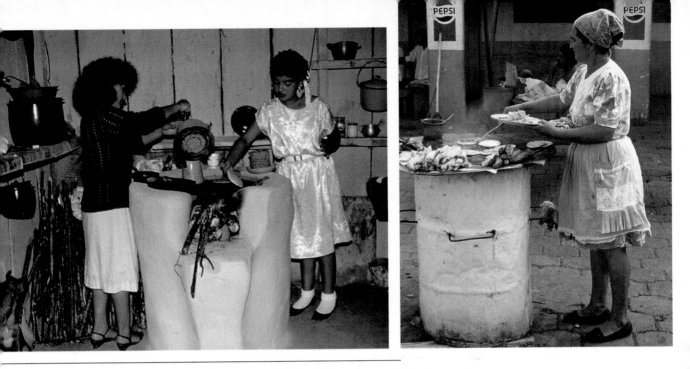

*Tortillas are cooked over a wood fire (left) and
a street vendor prepares a variety of fried food (right).*

FOODS

Hotels and restaurants cook many common foods, but with local styles and ingredients. Grilled steaks, pork chops, and chicken come with fried plantains (bananas), beans, and rice. Sauces almost always include garlic and onion. Vegetables that go with these dishes are *chayote* (vegetable pear) or *yuca* (cassava).

The most common food is the *tortilla*, a flat corn patty. Tortillas substitute for bread during a meal, with *tapado* (vegetable-meat soup) and *mondongo* (tripe soup). For most Hondurans tortillas and beans are the basis for every meal. Meat, milk, eggs, and other vegetables often cost too much. When there is money, rural Hondurans buy coffee, sugar, rice, bread, and cooking oil. Women cook *tamales*, which are made from tortillas or mashed corn dough and filled with meat and sauce. Street vendors sell tasty *baliadas*, tortillas filled with refried beans, cheese, or eggs.

Left: A wood-carver makes a figure out of mahogany.
Right: Colorful handcrafted baskets for sale

Food stands along the highway prepare pale, chewy field corn cooked in the husks over open fires. Peeled bananas and oranges are sold with salt and nutmeg for flavor. Papaya and other fruits are made into preserves for breakfast.

Black Caribs of the Bay Islands eat more seafood than is eaten elsewhere in Honduras. Shrimp and lobster are mixed with rice and coconut for many dishes. Coconut meat also is baked into local breads.

THE ARTS

Honduran art emphasizes handicrafts. The Comayaguela area of Tegucigalpa houses the *Mercado de Artesanias Populares*, the "Popular Artists Market." Leather goods, paintings by local artists, wood carvings, and textiles are sold.

Many of these artists train at *Valle de Angeles*, "Valley of the Angels," near Tegucigalpa. They learn wood carving, jewelry

An oil painting of a Honduran village by José Antonio Velásquez.

patterns, and wicker weaving in this seventeenth-century handicraft school. Some Honduran artists have earned worldwide recognition for their plastic sculptures. Painters José Antonio Velásquez and Roque Zelaya are well known for their brightly colored primitive artwork.

Small but active art communities always have existed in Honduras. Several authors gained popularity as revolutionary leaders as well as writers. José Cecilio Valle wrote the Central American Declaration of Independence. He later developed a reputation as a philosopher and scientist. Froylan Zamorano was a noted twentieth-century poet. More recently, Rafael Heliodoro Valle earned fame for his historic writings.

The National University was started by José Trinidad Reyes, a poet and playwright. He brought the first piano to Tegucigalpa in the early nineteenth century. The university continues to support artists with poetry readings, art exhibits, and musical programs.

Brightly costumed dancers (left)
The Honduran goalie Belarmino Rivera makes a save during
the 1991 Gold Cup soccer finals in Los Angeles.

RECREATION AND FESTIVALS

Futbol, or soccer, is a national sport. The National Stadium in
Tegucigalpa and the Morazán Stadium in San Pedro Sula hold
team matches. Smaller towns and villages provide their own
soccer fields where barefoot children play games before cheering
crowds.

Baseball is another popular sport along with water sports.
Snorkeling off the Bay Island coral reefs draws many city folk and
vacationing tourists to Honduras. The national pastime for adult
men, however, is billiards. Billiard halls offer a break from
backbreaking labor in almost every town and village.

Leisure time is a luxury for most rural Hondurans. Poorer
children have little playtime and even fewer toys. Most are too
busy working to play. Many villages hold dances on Saturday

night to celebrate the week's end. Guitar players strum rhythms in the village square. A *marimba* (a musical instrument with a keyboard like a xylophone) band plays for special events.

Religious services and celebrations provide breaks from work routines. At Sunday school, children sing songs and learn prayers. Occasionally, priests make *piñatas*, hollowed out forms filled with treats. Blindfolded children take turns swatting a piñata until it breaks, sending fruits and other treats to the ground while the children scramble for the goodies.

Fiestas provide the main form of entertainment in villages. National holidays are New Year's Day (January 1), Day of the Americas (April 14), Labor Day (May 1), Independence Day (September 15), Columbus Day (October 12), Armed Forces Day (October 21), and Christmas (December 24 and 25). All of Honduras honors the birth of the national hero, General Morazán, on October 3, the Day of Francisco Morazán.

Besides national holidays, every town holds its own local celebration. Most often, the holiday honors a patron saint. In eastern towns with Indian populations, fiestas follow colorful ancient customs. Other fiestas offer beauty contests, dances, and plenty of games.

Elaborate celebrations at Tela on the Caribbean occur during the holiday week before Easter. Families arrive in luxury cars and beat-up yellow school buses discarded by the United States. Vendors sell skewers of barbecued beef and cups of chopped ice flavored with pink and purple juices. Rich and poor, descendants of Africans, Indians, and Europeans wade into the sea as a beginning to the week of festivities. These tropical pleasures are free for every Honduran to enjoy.

Looking down on Tegucigalpa from Mount Picacho

Tegucigalpa

Chapter 8

TRAVELING THROUGH HONDURAS

Honduras is a country of contrasts. The landscape contains lush forested mountains in most places but bits of desert and savanna in others. Unspoiled beaches and hidden villages compete with industrial seaports, colonial cities, and ancient ruins. The untouched Mosquito Coast and Bay Islands contribute a flavor of their own. These are the many features of Honduras.

TEGUCIGALPA

Tegucigalpa is the largest and most populated city. More than 600,000 people live 3,000 feet (914 meters) up the slopes of Mount Picacho along the Choluteca River in south central Honduras. Tegucigalpa became the nation's capital in 1880. However, its origins date back more than 400 years.

Tegucigalpa started as a silver mining town in 1578 on September 29, St. Michael's Day. As it grew, the settlement was named *Real de Minas de San Miguel* in honor of the saint. *De Tegucigalpa*, meaning "of the silver hill" in the Nahuatl language, was added to separate the location from others named for the same saint. With time, the addition became the preferred name.

A view of Comayagua (left) from the tower of the Cathedral of Comayagua (right), which was started in 1685 and completed in 1715.

Tegucigalpa flourished as a mining center, while neighboring Comayaguela developed as the colonial capital. As Tegucigalpa grew in importance, the seat of government moved. Hondurans think of their capital as including Comayaguela. Together, they make up a combined metropolitan area of more than 700,000 people.

Tegucigalpa is a poor city. Yet it remains untouched by the earthquakes, fires, and volcanic explosions that plagued other early towns. Buildings, monuments, and parks display the country's heritage. Colonial styles mix with nineteenth-century and modern architecture. Tegucigalpa has lost its importance as the nation's foremost urban area, but it remains the heart of traditional Honduras.

Tegucigalpa streets wind through the city and climb the surrounding hills without any particular pattern. Streets and avenues are numbered rather than named. Pathways leading to

The National Congress building (left) and a house in the old section (right) of Tegucigalpa

hillside neighborhoods are too narrow and twisted for vehicles, and public stairways lend an old-world charm. Tegucigalpa is one of the few capitals in the world without a railroad. As modern times creep into the capital, asphalt replaces cobblestone streets, and concrete and glass buildings supplant colonial red tile roofs and pastel adobe houses.

Like most colonial cities Tegucigalpa has a city square, called Plaza Morazán. The square and nearby Central Park honor Francisco Morazán, the nineteenth-century hero of Central American unity, and an equestrian statue of Morazán stands in the park. Hondurans wander through the landscaped park night and day. Strollers buy gadgets for their children, munch on fast foods from street vendors, and enjoy the relaxed pace of the country.

The square is the site of many churches and government buildings. To the east is the Cathedral of Tegucigalpa, or San

Above: The Cathedral of San Miguel was completed in 1782.
Below: Herbs for sale in the market (left) and games and rides
for children (right) in "Fantasy Island."

Miguel. Construction of the twin-towered church lasted from 1756 to 1782. The church stands out for its unusual front pillars, which have grooves in the form of mermaids. Inside, the church houses an ornate golden pulpit and a handcrafted silver altar. The carvings are by Guatemalan sculptor Vincente Falez. Honduran José Miguel Gómez painted the surrounding religious scenes. These two men influenced religious art throughout the city.

On the south patio is a stone altar and a tree. Indians thought the tree sacred, and Spaniards called it the "Maternity Tree." Many births and weddings took place under its shade. Legend says that newlywed couples shook the tree for good luck, and the number of flowers that dropped foretold how many children they would have.

Nearby is the main commercial district. Modern hotels, restaurants, and banks line the street, which is closed to vehicles. Shops display every type of local handicraft, including pottery, textiles, leather goods, and beaded jewelry. Farther west is the Manuel Bonilla Theater, where Honduran artists perform on stage.

Residential neighborhoods and suburbs expand the city. Streets of elegant colonial homes mix with ordinary rows of two-story storefront buildings. Open markets and parks enclose smaller plazas. The capital experienced a population explosion during the 1980s. Now crowded dusty neighborhoods of shacks extend far into the scenic hillsides.

Comayaguela is an extension of Tegucigalpa now, and it is the place where workers live and labor. The area is southwest of downtown Tegucigalpa. The old capital has few of the sights and high-rise buildings that attract tourists to the current capital. Many merchants and craftspeople manage small businesses here. They sell their products in sprawling open-air stalls. The largest

The national stadium

market is the six-block San Isidro Market, where vendors sell items for everyday use. At the *Artesanias* "Handicraft" Market buyers find unusual folk arts, from mahogany wood carvings to baskets and hammocks.

Tegucigalpa is home to the national stadium and the country's museums. The National Museum of Anthropology and History has displays of Mayan and colonial Honduras. One of the most spectacular attractions, however, lies north of the city. United Nations Park stands 4,000 feet (1,219 meters) high on Mount Picacho, one of the many mountains surrounding the city. It offers a view of the entire valley and insight into what makes Honduras special.

San Pedro Sula

SAN PEDRO SULA

San Pedro Sula is Honduras's second, most-important city, with a population of more than 325,000, and the country's leading industrial center. San Pedro Sula's location in the north and at the heart of banana country along the Ulúa River has been the most important reason for its growth.

The city's roots go back to 1536, when Pedro de Alvarado founded the city as a Spanish military headquarters. Pirates, Indians, and later a yellow fever epidemic eventually destroyed the settlement. By the late 1870s, American companies planted bananas and developed the northern lowlands. Portions of an

A busy street (left) and an outdoor market (right) in San Pedro Sula

incomplete transcontinental railroad extended to San Pedro Sula.

Port facilities and roads brought new residents from the highlands and foreign countries. West Indian people from various Caribbean Island countries arrived to pick bananas on the enlarging plantations. Lebanese, who had migrated from their homeland to seek a living, entered the country as merchants. Today San Pedro Sula has citizens from several cultural backgrounds: Spanish, African, Lebanese, and mestizo. As each group arrived, food processing and construction industries developed. With time, the city expanded its economic and manufacturing base. San Pedro Sula soon outstripped the capital, Tegucigalpa, as a commercial center and became a trade route for distributing products to the north and west regions of Honduras.

This flat city is much more modern than the capital. A bus system, paved roads, and a railroad connect the many factories.

The Cathedral of San Pedro is built in the colonial style.

The airport serves other major parts of the country. High-rise buildings are less visible than in Tegucigalpa. San Pedro Sula claims a lively nightlife, with discos and restaurants. Honduras's second city is the fastest growing in the country.

NORTHERN PORT CITIES

Three leading port cities along the northern coasts are Puerto Cortés, Tela, and La Ceiba. Their ports and railroads continue to attract businesses and tourists. The voices of Chinese and Palestinian merchants mix with those of Spanish-speaking ladinos, Spanish- and English-speaking descendants of the West Indians, and Black Caribs seeking work in town. Tela was once the main port for the United Fruit Company. The company relocated after extensive crop rotation moved farms farther inland. Since then,

Freighters at anchor in Puerto Cortés

the company housing complex has been changed into a resort and the United Fruit experimental station into a botanical garden for tourists. The rest of Tela remains a smaller banana port town of clapboard houses, with beaches facing north and inland peaks of the *Nombre de Díos*, "Name of God," mountain range.

Thirty-one miles (fifty kilometers) west of Tela is Puerto Cortés, the largest port in Central America. The Spanish called the town *Puerto Caballos*, "Port of Horses," until 1869. Gil González Dávila named the port when he landed his ship during a storm. His cargo included seventeen horses, which he wanted to hide from the Indians. Never having encountered horses before, the Indians found the unusual animals mystical. González feared he would lose his hold over the Indians should the horses die like other creatures.

*Boxed bananas are moved from the railroad car
onto a cargo ship at La Ceiba port.*

Modern Puerto Cortés began on swampland across from Puerto Caballos as a terminal for the railway. The railroad project ended, but the port succeeded as a banana port and later a center for oil refining.

La Ceiba lies forty miles (sixty-four kilometers) east of Tela. The city's name comes from the broad ceiba trees that line a canal cutting through the town. This busy banana port has the largest population of the three ports and the most ships moving in and out of the harbor.

Much of the business comes from the Standard Fruit Company's claim to the town. La Ceiba is where Standard Fruit developed a type of banana that withstands Panama disease, a disease that commonly killed the fruit during the growing season. The

*A pineapple field near La Ceiba. Inset: Black Caribs
live on Roatán, the largest of the Bay Islands.*

company expanded fruit operations to include pineapple exports
under the brand name Dole.

Standard Fruit helped La Ceiba build a pleasant town. La
Ceiba's location makes it the gateway to the Bay Islands.

BAY ISLANDS

The Bay Islands are a string of eight undersea mountains
poking up from the floor of the Caribbean Sea. They cover an
area of about 92 square miles (238 square kilometers) located 38
miles (61 kilometers) off Honduras's northern shore. Eight major
islands and sixty-five smaller islets make up the Bay Islands. The
total population of the islands is about seventeen thousand
people.

The largest and most populated of the eight main islands is
Roatán. Other major settlements thrive on Utila and Guanaja.

The island of Utila (left) and the waiting room at the airport on Guanaja (right)

Several tiny coral islets mingle with the smaller islands of Morat, Santa Elena, and Barbareta.

The Bay Islands have been part of Honduras since 1859. But Spanish culture has little influence here. Bay Islanders lead much different lives from mainland inhabitants. Most speak English and were descended from African slaves or English pirates and fortune hunters. They make their living from fishing, turtle hunting, boating, and boatbuilding.

Many inland areas remain the same as in Columbus's time. Coconut palms and sea grape trees extend along the shores, and pine and oak tree jungles blanket most of the islands. Travel is mainly by boat. Roatán's airport runway can handle jets and Guanaja and Utila contain smaller airstrips. Timetables are of little importance on the islands, however. Telephones, clocks, facsimile (fax) machines, and television appeared only recently in resort hotels.

The Bay Islands are known for recreational diving. With a calm sea and warm water, the sea is perfect for underwater exploration. Coral reefs that surround each island descend twenty to forty feet (six to twelve meters). Beneath the sea are exciting caves and huge dropoffs, some as deep as one hundred to two hundred feet (thirty to sixty-one meters). Inland on Guanaja the scenery is equally rugged. Waterfalls abound and streams flow down the slopes of the higher mountains into the ocean.

Roatán is the only island with inland villages, at Corozal and Juticalpa. Otherwise, most of the twenty thousand Bay Islanders settle along the coast. Many live in white or brightly painted clapboard stilt houses with tin roofs. Black Carib villagers at Punta Gorda construct traditional homes on the ground with palm thatch for floors and roofs. Bananas, plantains, cassavas, and other produce come from the mainland on floating markets. Boaters dock their boats by shoreside villages to peddle their products.

LA MOSQUITIA OR MOSQUITO COAST

Tropical rain forests cover most of La Mosquitia, the Mosquito Coast. The area remains one of the most unoccupied regions of Honduras. A few small towns and Miskito Indian villages dot the jungles.

Until 1904 the Indians felt little loyalty to Honduras or Nicaragua. Both nations chose King Alfonso XIII of Spain to decide disputed boundaries between the two countries. After two years, Alfonso gave the questioned area to Honduras and set the Honduran-Nicaragua border along the Coco River.

Border conflicts flared from time to time. Miskito Indians from both countries, encouraged by the United States, fought against

Opposite page: The Bay Islands are excellent for underwater exploration, with exotic coral reefs and beautifully colored fish. Inset: A view of Roatán

Copán was a thriving community from about A.D. 450 to A.D. 800.

the Nicaraguan government during the 1980s. Originally Nicaraguan soldiers tried to remove the Indians from border villages. Later the Nicaraguan government changed its policy and began to encourage increased political independence for Miskito Indians. Large numbers of Miskito refugees from Nicaragua sought shelter within Honduras, causing problems for the already poor country.

COPÁN

Copán is the site of the most important ancient ruins in Honduras. The ruins are 140 miles (225 kilometers) from Tegucigalpa and 120 miles (193 kilometers) from San Pedro Sula. They spread over a forested valley in the western mountains that rise 2,100 feet (640 meters) above sea level. Travelers can walk to the ruins from town over unpaved, bumpy roads. Isolated Indian settlements nearby remain locked in the past.

Maya sculpture in Copán

Other Mayan ruins in Mexico and Guatemala expose grander structures. Copán, however, reveals more monuments than any other Mayan city. These monuments display the most elaborate decorations produced by the Maya anywhere. Artists of the day competed to carve their deeds in pictures, hieroglyphs, and swirls. Hieroglyphs covered temples, stairways, and tall limestone *stelae* (carved pillars made to commemorate events). Through the years, archaeologists have decoded many of the hieroglyphs. They disclose Copán's importance as the champion of Mayan art and astronomy.

Historians believe that Copán was settled about 2000 B.C. The fertile valley had good soil for growing corn. At first, the Maya built only simple thatch houses. As the Maya developed, they

Archaeologists are attempting to restore parts of Copán.

began to build major monuments and temples of stone and volcanic rock. Common clay and wooden tools became fancier, decorated objects. Rulers began the custom of recording their history on buildings, monuments, and tombs.

When the Maya declined, they left many accounts of the past carved into these stone monuments. The main ceremonial center at Copán covers about 75 acres (30 hectares). A temple stairway of 62 steps shows more than 1,250 hieroglyphs that record the history of Copán royalty. Residential and administrative buildings surround the center. Other detailed temples and monuments sprinkle the slopes of the valley.

Copán is still an archaeological site. Workers from the Honduran Institute of Archaeology and History section off areas regularly. They perform the delicate job of unearthing remains with shovels, dental picks, and brushes.

Nearby is Copán Ruinas, a small town that got its name from the ruins 0.6 mile (1 kilometer) away. Down the cobblestone streets on the town square is the Museo Copán. The museum

Modern and ancient citizens of Honduras

houses a collection of Mayan artifacts taken from the ruins. Displays show jade, shell, and bone jewelry from royalty and objects from tombs. One tomb contains clay figures and a skull that has a tooth with a jade filling. Another museum and visitor center is under construction nearby. The museum will explain the wonders of the early Mayan people and how their legacy became the Honduras of today.

A COUNTRY TO REMEMBER

After traveling through Honduras, visitors understand more about the beauty of its landscape, the richness of its history, and, sadly, the mixture of wealth and poverty of its people. Before the 1980s Honduras was unknown country to outsiders. Since then, the nation has been a site for international political schemes and military activity. But a deeper study of Honduran history, government, and culture suggests that there is much more to value in this country than the fact that foreigners moved armies onto its soil.

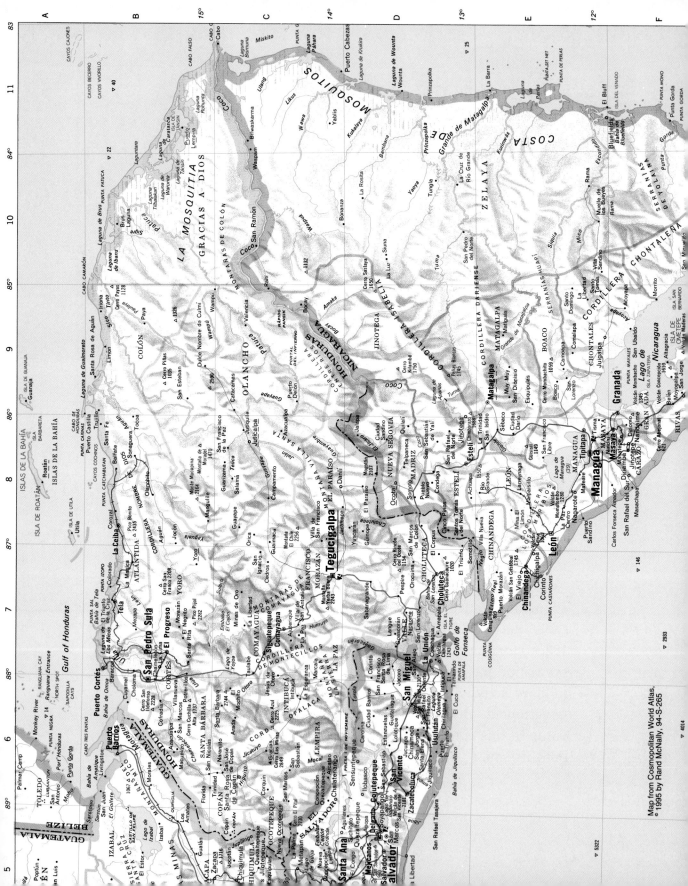

Map from Cosmopolitan World Atlas, ©1995 by Rand McNally, 94-S-265

MAP KEY

MINI-FACTS AT A GLANCE

GENERAL INFORMATION

Official Name: *República de Honduras* (Republic of Honduras)

Capital: Tegucigalpa. According to the constitution, Tegucigalpa and the adjacent city of Comayaguela jointly form the capital.

Government: Honduras is a multiparty republic with one legislative house, the Congress. The president of the republic is elected every four years and controls the legislative and judicial branches of the government. As head of state and government, the president selects people to fill all public posts including members of the cabinet. Historically, the Honduran army has been powerful in the decision-making process, and military leaders can veto any of the presidential appointments to the cabinet. The legal system is based on Roman and Spanish civil law, with some influence of English common law. The Supreme Court consists of nine members, but the court changes with each new government. For administrative purposes the country is divided into 18 departments.

Religion: The constitution does not support any religion, but guarantees freedom of religion to all. Almost 83 percent of the population follows Roman Catholicism. Protestants, mostly fundamentalists such as Moravian and Methodist, make up some 12 percent of the population. Black Caribs, or *Garífuna*, are also Catholics but follow many customs from their African origins.

Ethnic Composition: Almost 90 percent of the population is of mestizo origin, followed by Amerindian 6.5 percent, Black Carib 2 percent, and white 1.5 percent. Mestizos are people of mixed Spanish and Indian ancestry. Amerindians are divided into two larger groups of either Lenca or Chorti. Miskito and Sumos Indians live in forested northeastern Honduras. There are some Arab-speaking Christian immigrants from the Middle East, especially from Lebanon.

Language: Spanish is the official language. Black Carib people speak an Arawak Indian language and the Pipil speak the Nahuatl language.

National Flag: The flag consists of a white horizontal stripe between two blue horizontal stripes; five blue stars on the white stripe represent the five members of the former union of Central American provinces.

National Emblem: The emblem consists of an oval shield with a stone pyramid surrounded by blue skies and a blue sea; the shield is bordered with a white band inscribed with the name of the country, the date of independence, and the national motto, *Libre, Soberana e Independiente*, "Free, Sovereign and Independent." The shield is embraced by two cornucopias spilling roses. The emblem rests on a brown mound along with a farmhouse, farm tools, and trees.

National Anthem: *"Himno Nacional de Honduras"* ("National Hymn of Honduras")

National Calendar: Gregorian

Money: Honduran *lempira* (L) of 100 centavos is the official currency. In 1995 one lempira was worth $0.09 in United States currency.

Membership in International Organizations: Central American Common Market (CACM), International Bank for Reconstruction and Development (IBRD), World Bank, International Monetary Fund (IMF), Organization of American States (OAS), United Nations (UN)

Weights and Measures: The metric system is in force. Some old Spanish measures also are in use.

Population: 5,783,000 in 1994; 134 persons per sq. mi.; 52 persons per sq km; 48 percent urban; 52 percent rural

Cities:

Tegucigalpa	608,100
San Pedro Sula	300,900
La Ceiba	71,600
El Progreso	63,400
Choluteca	57,400
Comayagua	39,600
Puerto Cortés	32,000
Danli	31,100
Siguatepeque	28,900
Tela	23,600
Juticalpa	20,600
Santa Rosa de Copán	20,300
Olancho	14,600

(Population based on 1989 estimates.)

GEOGRAPHY

Border: Honduras is the second largest of the seven Central American countries. Nicaragua is to the south, Guatemala is to the northwest, and El Salvador is to the southwest.

Coastline: The Caribbean coastline in the north is about 382 mi. (615 km) long and the Pacific coastline in the southwest along the Gulf of Fonseca is 48 mi. (77 km) long.

Land: The five main geographical regions are the interior highlands, the Pacific lowlands, the Caribbean lowlands, the Mosquito Coast (called after the Miskito Indian tribe) in the northeast, and a number of small islands in the Caribbean Sea and the Gulf of Fonseca. Thick rain forests cover most of the interior highlands, but the region supports about three-fourths of the total Honduran population. The lowlands are confined to the coastal plains and river valleys and are not very wide. The Mosquito Coast is one of the most unoccupied regions of Honduras; only a few small Indian towns populate this area. Bay Islands are a string of eight undersea mountains poking up from the floor of the Caribbean Sea.

Almost 80 percent of Honduras is mountainous. The three main mountain ranges include the Cordillera Opalaca in the west, Montañas de Comayagua in the south-central region, and Montañas del Patuca reaching eastward. Unlike other Central American countries, Honduras has no active volcanoes.

Highest Point: Cerros de Celaque, 9,400 ft. (2,865 m)

Lowest Point: Sea level along the coasts

Rivers: There are many rivers, streams, and coastal lagoons with coral reefs. Major rivers are the Ulúa, Goascoran, Choluteca, Nacaome, Coco, and Patuca. The Patuca River is known for its waterfalls. Rivers sometimes provide travel facility in areas where there are few roads. Several waterways are navigable for small ships. Situated at the height of 2,100 ft. (640 m), Lake Yojoa is 12 mi. (19 km) long and 7 mi. (11 km) wide.

Forests: Almost 30 percent of the area is under forests. Mountain slopes are covered with ferns, mosses, wild avocados, and rare orchids. Lowland regions grow mahogany, silk cotton, Spanish cedar, rosewood, palm, and pine. Mangroves occupy the country's low coastal swamps; acacias and cactus bloom in the drier regions.

Wildlife: Wildlife includes anteaters, armadillos, coyotes, deer, raccoons, turkeys, pumas, coatis, sloths, snakes, crocodiles, caymans, turtles, manatees, and salamanders. Ocean life includes mollusks, snails, lobsters, shrimp, and crabs. Fish and turtles are abundant in both freshwater and marine varieties. The Lancetilla Botanical Garden preserves most bird species found in the country. The quetzal is a rare bird with long tail feathers; other special birds found are the black robin, wood hewer, clorospinga, motmot, curassow, hummingbird, wild hen, macaws, nightingale, and tanamou.

Climate: The northern and southern coastal plains have a wet, tropical climate, but the interior is drier and cooler. Lowland temperatures are always hot while the highland regions have milder weather. There are two major seasons—the rainy season from May to October and a dry season from November to April. The average annual rainfall varies from over 95 in. (240 cm) along the northern coast to about 33 in. (84 cm) in the south. Tropical rain forests receive more than 100 in. (254 cm) of rain per year. Hurricanes are a continual problem, especially on the northwest coast.

Greatest Distance: East to West: 405 mi. (652 km)
North to South: 240 mi. (386 km)

Area: 43,277 sq. mi. (112,088 sq km)

ECONOMY AND INDUSTRY

Agriculture: Because of the mountainous terrain, Honduras has less land available for farming than any other Central American country. The land distribution is very uneven—almost half of the agricultural land is owned by less than 5 percent of the people. Less than 50 percent of the people own land for farming. Foreign companies still control vast areas of banana plantations. Bananas are the chief export crop, followed by coffee. Other crops include corn, cotton, sugarcane, rice, and tobacco. Recently the government has tried to diversify agricultural production by investing in crops such as pineapples, melons, spices, vegetables, and flowers. Farmers grow lemons, oranges, grapefruit, and pineapples in the northern coastal region for export.
The coastal lowlands have rich savanna pastures; these grasslands are valuable for raising livestock. More than one-fourth of fertile land is used for raising beef and dairy cattle. Lobster and shrimp are important sea products. Shrimp farming occurs mainly in the Gulf of Fonseca and on the North Coast.

Mining: The mineral resource base is small; there are small deposits of lead, zinc, tin, iron, coal, antimony, silver, marble, gypsum, and limestone. Most electrical energy comes from imported oil and hydroelectric power.

Manufacturing: Manufacturing accounts for about 16 percent of the Honduran economy and employs about 9 percent of the workforce. There is an oil refinery in Puerto Cortés that processes unrefined foreign oil. There are hydroelectric plants at Río Lindo, El Nispers, and El Cajon. Other manufactured items include clothing and textiles, plastic, cement, soap, rubber, footwear, cigarettes, lumber, processed foods, and beverages. Farm-related industries include meat packing, sugar mills, furniture factories, and paper plants. *Maquiladoras* are government-sponsored factories that are built by local developers but leased to foreign companies. Several US companies manufacture furniture in Honduras.

Transportation: Honduran railways are largely operated by the fruit companies. There are some 583 mi. (939 km) of railroads. The Inter-Ocean Highway links the cities of Tegucigalpa and San Pedro Sula. The total length of roads is about 7,066 mi. (11,371 km); few of the rural roads are paved. Several airfields and military bases were built across Honduras by the United States army. Two international airports are at Tegucigalpa and San Pedro Sula. Puerto Cortés is the largest port in Central America. La Ceiba is also a busy banana port.

Communication: There are five daily newspapers including *La Tribuna*, *El Tiempo*, and *La Prensa*. Postal, telephone, and telegraph services are owned and operated by the government. All broadcasts are in Spanish. In the early 1990s there was one radio receiver per 3 persons; one television set per 31 persons, and one telephone per 46 persons. There is no national film industry.

Trade: The chief imports are machinery and transport equipment, mineral fuels, chemical products, plastics and resins, and metals. Major import sources are the United States, Japan, Mexico, Venezuela, and the Netherlands. Chief export items are bananas, coffee, shrimp and lobsters, lead, zinc, and timber. Major export destinations are the United States, Germany, Belgium, Japan, and Italy.

EVERYDAY LIFE

Health: Health conditions in Honduras are among the least developed in the Central American countries. Rural health clinics have an acute shortage of doctors, medicine, and equipment. The major health problems are malnutrition, gastritis, enteritis, malaria, whooping cough, typhoid fever, and tuberculosis. People in general lack the vitamins for good health. Life expectancy at 63 years for males and 67 years for females is low. Infant mortality rate at 70 per 1,000 is high even when compared to other Latin American nations.

Education: Primary education is compulsory and is provided free of charge, but many children do not go to school; household work and frequent illness cause children to miss classes. There is a serious shortage of schools and teachers in rural areas. Primary education starts at seven years of age and lasts for six years. Secondary education starts at the age of 13 years and lasts for six years. On completion of the compulsory period of primary education, every person is required to teach at least two illiterate adults to read and write. The Catholic Church operates private schools in the cities. The National Autonomous University of Honduras is at Tegucigalpa; it has branch campuses in San Pedro Sula and La Ceiba. There are three additional private universities. The Pan American Agricultural School and the Francisco Morazán Military Academy are near the capital. In the early 1990s the literacy rate was about 56 percent.

Holidays:
New Year's Day, January 1
Pan American Day/Day of the Americas, April 14
Labor Day, May 1
Independence Day, September 15
Francisco Morazán Day, October 3
Columbus Day, October 12
Army Day, October 21
King Alfonso's Decision Day, December 18
Christmas, December 25

Movable religious holidays include Holy Thursday, Good Friday, Holy Saturday, and Easter.

Culture: Honduran culture has been strongly influenced by the country's Spanish cultural heritage. The National Museum of Anthropology and History at Tegucigalpa displays Mayan and Colonial Honduran objects. The Museo Copán houses a collection of Mayan artifacts of clay figures and jade, shell, and bone jewelry. The noted Mayan ruins at Copán—the second largest city of the Mayan Empire—have been largely rebuilt and restored by the government in an attempt to attract foreign tourists. Handicrafts include leather goods, paintings by local artists, mahogany wood carvings, jewelry, wicker weaving, and textiles.

Society: Most of the Hondurans are *campesinos* or rural peasants. They live in villages away from the main roads. Honduras has one of the stronger women's movements in Central America. Married and single women are responsible for the children and household. Almost half the households are headed by women. They wake up before dawn to grind the corn for tortillas—a round flat bread—and prepare coffee. Children accompany their mothers into the mountains to gather firewood for cooking and help in the fields by digging, plowing, and chopping wood.

Dress: Most of the Hondurans wear Western style clothing in urban areas. Chorti Indian men wear traditional white shirts and pants, and women wear long skirts and short blouses.

Housing: The one-room rural homes, called *ranchos*, are made of bamboo, sugarcane, or corn stalks and mud; roofs are made of tightly sewn cane. A piece of cloth hangs from the ceiling to divide the room. Wood-burning stoves are used in the kitchen; beds are mats on the floor or hammocks. Tree stumps are generally used for sitting. Some urban houses have cement floors and tiled roofs. Larger towns have electricity and running water.

Food: Corn, rice, and beans are three staple foods for rural Hondurans. Corn is eaten in the form of tortillas or *tamales* (ground corn cakes). Wealthier Hondurans eat pork, beef, eggs, and a variety of tropical fruits and vegetables. Meat dishes are served with fried plantains, beans, and rice. *Tapado* is a vegetable-meat soup. Roadside food stands sell field corn cooked in its husk over open fires and peeled bananas and oranges with salt and nutmeg. Fish dishes are popular on the Caribbean Coast. The national drink is coffee.

Sports and Recreation: *Futbol* or soccer is the national sport. The National Stadium is in Tegucigalpa and the Morazán Stadium is in San Pedro Sula. Baseball is another popular sport. The national pastime for adult Honduran men is billiards. Many villages hold dances on Saturday night to celebrate the week's end. Fiestas provide the main form of entertainment in villages. A *marimba* band plays for special events.

The Bay Islands are known for recreational diving for underwater exploration; Roatán Island offers an opportunity to observe how dolphins behave in their natural setting.

Social Welfare: The government-run system of social security provides benefits for sickness, maternity, orphans, unemployment, and accidents. It also provides family and old-age allowances. Private social welfare organizations include Catholic charities.

IMPORTANT DATES

1502—Christopher Columbus arrives at the port of Trujillo

1522—Permanent settlement by Europeans begins

1526—The first territorial governor is appointed

1536—San Pedro Sula is founded as a Spanish military headquarters

1537—A major war breaks out between the Indians and the Spaniards

1570—Honduras becomes part of the Captaincy General of Guatemala

1578—Silver deposits near Tegucigalpa are discovered

1821—Mexico announces its independence from Spain; a group in Guatemala City declares all of Central America independent of Spain

1823—Central American states form their own confederation without Mexico

1824—The constitution of the United Provinces of Central America is created

1826—Conservatives gain power in governing the United Provinces

1838—Honduras leaves the federation of the United Provinces of Central America and declares independence

1839—Honduras adopts its first constitution; the United Provinces comes to an end

1847—The National Autonomous University of Honduras is founded at Tegucigalpa

1859—The Bay Islands become part of Honduras

1863—The Swan Islands are taken over by the United States to exploit guano

1866—Honduras adds a group of five blue stars to its flag to express a hope for a new federation of Central America in the future

1869—Name for Puerto Caballos is changed to Puerto Cortés

1876—Conservatives lose political power to the liberals

1880—Tegucigalpa becomes the nation's capital; the National Archives of Honduras is established

1891—The modern Liberal Party begins operation

1892—Outbreak of yellow fever closes businesses for months

1899—The first boatload of bananas is sent to Louisiana

1904—The Standard Fruit Company is started by the Vaccaro brothers; King Alfonso XIII of Spain settles the boundary between Honduras and Nicaragua along the Coco River

1911—The Cuyamel Fruit Company is started

1927—The modern conservative party, called the National Party, begins operation

1930—Honduras is the world's leading banana producer

1932—General Tiburcio Carías Andino is elected president

1933—Border issue with Guatemala is settled

1942—The Pan American Agricultural School is founded by the United Fruit Company

1948—President Carías steps down after a 16-year rule; Honduras holds its first free election in 16 years; Manuel Gálvez is elected president

1949—Present design of the national flag is adopted

1954—Honduras suffers its first general strike; the strike started the tradition of a strong labor movement that continues to defend worker rights today; women are given the right to vote

1957—The National Assembly drafts a new constitution; a new labor code and social security law are adopted

1959—Television is introduced

1960—The International Court of Justice awards the disputed land between Nicaragua and Honduras to Honduras

1963—President Ramón Villeda Morales is deposed in an army coup

1965—A new constitution is promulgated to replace the 1957 constitution

1969—Soccer riots spark a four-day war between El Salvador and Honduras; the Organization of American States (OAS) steps in to end the fighting; Honduras suspends participation in the Central American Common Market; a land reform law forces many Salvadorans living in Honduras to give up their land

1974—Hurricane Fifi kills 10,000 people and makes some 150,000 people homeless; property damage is about $1,000,000

1975—Banana bribe scandal rocks the Honduran government

1976—Border conflicts with El Salvador

1978—A three-man army junta is set up to rule the country

1980—Elections are held for the National Assembly; Honduras and Nicaragua sign an agreement to end their border dispute

1981—The Liberal Party wins in general elections; Roberto Suazo Córdova becomes president; a tourist complex is completed in the San Pedro Sula/Tela region

1982—A new constitution is promulgated

1984—The Family Code is passed giving rights to children in homes with single mothers

1985—National elections are held; José Azcona del Hoyo becomes president

1986—Border clashes between Honduras and Nicaragua

1987—Honduras participates and signs the Central American peace plan for the region

1988—The Contras, rebels from Nicaragua, and Sandinista government sign a cease-fire agreement

1989—Rafael Leonardo Callejas is elected president

1991—Honduras and El Salvador sign an agreement to establish a free trade zone on their common border

1992—The National Banana Council is formed to boost banana production and exports; a Pan American Health Organization study finds Honduran health services among the worst in the Western Hemisphere

1993—The Honduran military agrees to open its secret files to civilian authorities in connection with human rights violations in the 1980s

1994—Carlos Roberto Reina is sworn in as president

IMPORTANT PEOPLE

Pedro de Alvarado (c. 1485-1541), Spanish military leader; founded the town of San Pedro Sula

Manuel Arce (? -1847), president; former liberal who later became a conservative; sent army in 1826 into Honduras to crush a liberal revolt

Colonel Osvaldo López Arellano, military leader; overthrew the government in 1963 and became president; he became president again in 1972 until 1975

Policarpo Bonilla (1858-1926), author and politician

General Tiburcio Carías Andino (1876-1969), National Party member, elected president in 1932; he ended popular elections and ruled as head of military until 1948

José Rafael Carrera (1814-65), led a revolt against the United Provinces

Vincente Falez, Guatemalan sculptor; worked on the detailed carvings for the Cathedral of Tegucigalpa

Manuel Gálvez (1883-1962), president; replaced General Andino in 1948; created a national bank, and built roads and other public projects

Carlos Garay, landscape artist

José Miguel Gómez (1858-1921), artist; painted the religious scenes at the Cathedral of Tegucigalpa

Gil González Dávila (1578-1658), Spanish military leader; named the port city of Puerto Cortés as Puerto Caballos

Lempira (1497-1537), Lenca Indian who led one of the largest rebellions in Central America from 1537 to 1539; the Honduran national currency is named after him

Alberto Membreno (1859-1921), philologist

Juan Ramón Molina (1875-1908), modernist poet

Francisco Morazán (1799-1842), national hero of Honduras, the last president of the United Provinces of Central America, which lasted from 1823 to 1839; fought 21 battles from 1827 until 1839 to keep Central America united

Visitacíon Padilla, one of the early organizers of Women's Cultural Society; worked to gain rights for families on banana plantations and mine workers

José Trinidad Reyes (1797-1855), poet and playwright; founded an institute in 1847 that later became the National University

Ramón Rosa (1848-1930), writer and biographer

Marco Aurelio Soto (1846-1908), essayist and political leader

Clementina Suarez, poet

Froilan Turcios (1875-1943), novelist

Vaccaro brothers of New Orleans, Louisiana; they shipped the first boatload of bananas from Honduras to New Orleans; they also started the Standard Fruit Company in 1904

José Antonio Velásquez (1906-), artist, known for his brightly colored primitive artwork; he founded the National School of Arts and Crafts

José Cecilio del Valle (1780-1834), member of the French Academy of Sciences; intellectual and political leader; he wrote the Central American Declaration of Independence

Rafael Heliodoro Valle (1891-1959), poet, biographer, and historian

Ramón Villeda Morales (1909-71), physician turned president; he established the idea of public schools in 1957 and pushed for changes in education policies in the country's constitution

Froylan Zamorano, noted twentieth-century poet

Roque Zelaya, artist, known for his brightly colored artwork

Sam Zemurray (1877-1961), also known as Sam "the banana man" Zemurray; started the Cuyamel Company in 1911; later became president of the United Fruit Company in 1929 from which he retired in 1950

Compiled by Chandrika Kaul

INDEX

Page numbers that appear in boldface type indicate illustrations

About the Authors

Marlene Targ Brill is a free-lance Chicago-area writer, specializing in fiction and nonfiction books, articles, media, and other educational materials for children and adults. Among her credits are *John Adams* and *I Can Be a Lawyer* for Childrens Press; *Allen Jay and the Underground Railroad*, published by Carolrhoda Books; and *The Trail of Tears: A Journey from Home*, published by Millbrook Press.

Ms. Brill holds a B.A. in special education from the University of Illinois and an M.A. in early childhood education from Roosevelt University. She currently writes for readers of all ages who like to travel to new places and times through books.

Ms. Brill has written *Libya*, *Mongolia*, and *Algeria* in the Enchantment of the World series. She would like to thank her husband, Richard, and her brother, Harry Targ—her two geography and history consultants.

Harry B. Targ is a professor of political science and American studies at Purdue University in West Lafayette, Indiana. He has written and edited books and articles on United States foreign policy, United States political economy, Nicaragua, and Cuba. Mr. Targ's book *People's Nicaragua* was published in 1989; another book, *Cuba and the USA: A New World Order?*, was published in 1992. *Plant Closings: International Context and Social Costs*, written with Carolyn Perrucci, Robert Perrucci, and Dena B. Targ, was published in 1988.

The Brill-Targ collaboration also has produced *Guatemala* in the Enchantment of the World series.

Professor Targ received an M.A. in political science from the University of Illinois and a Ph.D. in political science from Northwestern University.

Professor Targ affirms his love for Dena Targ, Rebecca Targ, and Genevieve Targ. Marlene Targ Brill, his sister, is not so bad either.